The Secrets of Great Sales Management

The Secrets of Great Sales Management

Advanced Strategies for Maximizing Performance

Robert A. Simpkins

American Management Association

New York • Atlanta • Brussels • Chicago • Mexico City • San Francisco
Shanghai • Tokyo • Toronto • Washington, D.C.

Special discounts on bulk quantities of AMACOM books are available to corporations, professional associations, and other organizations. For details, contact Special Sales Department, AMACOM, a division of American Management Association, 1601 Broadway, New York, NY 10019.
Tel.: 212-903-8316. Fax: 212-903-8083.
Web site: www.amacombooks.org

This publication is designed to provide accurate and authoritative information in regard to the subject matter covered. It is sold with the understanding that the publisher is not engaged in rendering legal, accounting, or other professional service. If legal advice or other expert assistance is required, the services of a competent professional person should be sought.

Library of Congress Cataloging-in-Publication Data

Simpkins, Robert A., 1945–
  The secrets of great sales management : advanced strategies for maximizing performance / Robert A. Simpkins.
   p. cm.
  Includes index.
  ISBN 0-8144-7238-9 (hardcover)
  1. Sales management. 2. Sales personnel—Training of. I. Title.

HF5438.4.S52 2004
658.8′1—dc22

                   2004004340

Printing number

10 9 8 7 6 5 4 3 2 1

This book is dedicated to my father, the finest salesperson I have ever known. He taught me from the beginning that selling is all about the respect and dignity of people.

Contents

Acknowledgments xi

Introduction 1

I. PLANNING 7

Chapter 1: The Changing World of Sales Management 9
    What's Expected of You? 14
    Knowing the Business Realities: Situational Analysis 16
    Customer Values Benchmarking 20
    Developing Critical Objectives 22

Chapter 2: Planning for Today *and* Tomorrow 27
    The Value of Planning 29
    A Snapshot of Today 30
    Scenario and Simulation Planning 38
    Determining Prioritized Corporate Objectives 41
    Clarifying Short-Term, Intermediate, and Long-Term
        Goals 43
    Creating Directional Statements for Your Sales Team 46
    Determining Resource Requirements and
        Availability 48

Chapter 3: Crafting the Professional Sales Force 53
  Setting Out Your Goals 55
  Establishing Performance Objectives and
    Measurements 56
  Raising the Bar for Existing Sales Team Members . . . 65
  Using the New Performance Standards to Hire 66

II. PREPARING 69

Chapter 4: Finding the Talent 71
  Recruiting and Hiring Practices 73
  How to Recruit 79
  Interviewing "Best Practices" 80
  Understanding the Legal and Ethical Ramifications
    of Recruiting and Hiring 86

Chapter 5: Strengthening the Sales Team 91
  The Strong Grow Stronger 93
  Linking Organizational Processes 94
  Selecting and Implementing Critical Technologies . . 95
  Understanding Evolving Technologies and Software   96
  Using Technology as a Point of Differentiation. 102
  Effective Development and Training Initiatives 103
  Determining Strengths and Weaknesses of Individual
    Sales Team Members 104
  Creating Individualized Plans for Growth 105
  Getting the Sales Professional's "Buy-In" 107

**Chapter 6: Compensation Programs That Drive
Superior Performance** 111
  Sales Force Compensation 113
  Making Sure Your Compensation Plan Drives the
    Desired Objectives 116
  Weighing Compensation Plan Variations 119

Watching for Negative Results 123
Fine-Tuning the Plan 126
Making the Plan Fair for Everyone 128

III. PRODUCING 131

**Chapter 7: Now Lead: Measuring and Managing
Performance** 133
Sales Forecasting 135
Performance Evaluations 136
Understanding Changes in the Territories and the
    Marketplace That Impact Performance 143
Recognizing Individual Challenges 153
Identifying All Contributors to a Forecast 154
Communicating the Results to Senior Management   155

Chapter 8: Coaching and Counseling 159
The Art of Coaching 161
Coaching Skills to Improve Performance 163
The Ride-Along or Co-Calling Coaching Session 164
The Office Coaching Session 168
Creating a Motivational Environment 173
Dealing with the Difficult Times 176
Counseling the Problem Team Member 177
Managing Dismissals Intelligently 178
Legal Considerations 179

Chapter 9: Looking Toward the Future 181
Creating Career Development Plans for Your Sales
    Team Members 184
Matching the Plan to Goals 184
Preparing for Turnover 188
Succession and Legacy Planning 189
Wearing the Mantle of Leadership 191

Conclusion 197

A Leadership Growth Plan 201

A Checklist for Success 203

Index 207

Acknowledgments

First and foremost, I will always be indebted to Behnaz S. Paknejad, my treasured business partner for the last eight years. Besides leading Global Crosswinds, our advisory and training organization, as our chief operating officer, day in and day out, she added invaluable philosophical insights and content to this book (and laboriously edited every word).

Also, I would like to thank each of the following individuals for their support, enthusiasm, friendship, and leadership during my career: John Berndt, Gary Ring, and Robert Condon for their willingness to tap into my creativity and allow it to blossom; the late Tom Phelan, my first sales manager, for his kindness and patience; and David Knight, a business and personal friend for over twenty years. In addition, I would like to thank Richard Tyrrell for encouraging me to the write this book and Ellen R. Kadin, senior acquisitions editor, and Erika Spelman, associate editor, at AMACOM, for their sponsorship and support in bringing this book to fruition. What a lifetime of teamwork.

I would especially like to thank Linda, Erik, and Kristen for their support and encouragement, and my wonderful, beautiful grandchildren, Lauren, Brandon, and Jordan for giving me the reason to write this book.

Introduction

This book is written as a celebration. What are we celebrating? We're taking some time to acknowledge, appreciate, and honor the amazing accomplishments and hard work that have placed you in a position of sales team leadership for your organization. Long hours and, at times, frustrating work have finally led to your being responsible not only for the success of your sales professionals, but for the success of the organization. If your team doesn't sell, those across the organizational value chain have nothing to gather raw input for, add value to, distribute out, or service. Without you and your team, the equipment will be turned off, the doors shuttered, and the employee base unemployed. Feeling the pressure yet?

When I was a very young boy, growing toward adolescence in Alhambra, California, I had the opportunity to spend some time "hanging out" in my father's printing business. I felt as if I were working, but the reality is that I was probably just adding gray hair to my father's head. As is typical of most small businesses, my father and his associates spent the nor-

1

mal working hours selling and the after hours producing what would be sold the next day. Sometimes I had the chance to ride around with my dad as he made sales calls. People always seemed to be glad to see him, and we often got to have lighthearted lunch breaks. The impression left on a little boy was that selling was calling on friends and having chili dogs. Can you think of a better way to spend a career?

During that youthful period of my life, I encountered an event that changed my life forever. I know that the important cast of actors in this event probably don't recall it, but I have never forgotten it.

On the street where I was raised, there was one giant avocado tree behind a vacant house. Anyone who knows the southern California state of mind knows how this unique produce is valued for a multitude of tasteful uses. Even though the house was vacant, the aged tree kept producing wonderful, thick-skinned delicacies. The neighbors would occasionally go into the backyard and see if there were any avocados that were ready to pick from a low-hanging branch or that had recently fallen to the ground. In either case, there would be wonderful additions to someone's dinner table that night.

All this came to a halt one day when a family bought the house and moved in. Fortunately for me, the family had a young boy of my age who became a close friend for many years. One day, as we were out fooling around in the back-yard, I noticed his mother casually picking up the fallen avo-cados and unceremoniously tossing them into the trash can. "How could she do that?" I asked my friend and got an an-swer that shocked me. With a facial expression to emphasize the point, he informed me that his family hated them. Once enough time had passed for his response to sink in, a thought popped into my head. As the son of a salesman, I suggested we sell them to the neighbors.

That's when I got my first lesson in sales. Dennis, my friend, said in no uncertain terms that he had no intention of trying to sell to the neighbors. I can't recall exactly what he said, but I recognized terror when I heard it. He could not visualize himself going up to doors and talking semistrangers into giving him money for something that grew in his own backyard. What I found out, at a very early age, was that selling was not for everyone! Some people just don't feel comfortable with the whole process. If I had agreed, there would be no story to tell. But, being the son of a salesperson, I overcame this objection with an idea. We would load up my friend's wagon with avocados, and I would sell them to the neighbors. In essence, Dennis would pull the wagon and I would go door-to-door. Since we would split the proceeds, Dennis thought he was getting the better part of the deal, and I thought I was.

All day we became a sales channel for a desired product. As the sun set on our first day, we had sold every avocado we could get our hands on. The funny thing is that I can't remember what I did with my share of the proceeds. I probably spent it on soft drinks and comic books. It turned out, interestingly enough, that the sales activity was the highlight of the day for me. That evening, I returned home and proudly detailed the activity to my dad. I was excited that my first selling effort had been a success and that I had actually created the sales job. My father was great. He listened patiently to my story, and then added a single statement that left an impact on me for the rest of my life. He said, "Son, if you can sell, there will always be someone to pull the wagon."

Wow! Of course, as a youngster, it took some time for that to sink in. He didn't say it was *my* wagon. He said *the* wagon. He was referring to all those talented people who design, engineer, purchase, receive, inventory, advertise, manufacture, assemble, package, ship, and service a company's offerings. Because you have strong selling capabilities, they enthusiastically load up the wagon with wonderful, and much needed, products and services if you and your team will just go out and knock on the doors of strangers who will give the organization money for its creativity and hard work.

So up to here, this story makes it sound as if the world of commerce has a nice division of labor. But alas, all is not that easy in the world of sellers and wagon pullers. As the pace of business continues to speed up, the consequences of what a sales organization does—or does not—do carries an increasing level of importance. In the past, a sales strategy or focus could be delineated and adhered to for a measurable period of time, such as a calendar or fiscal year. If the program failed to meet organizational objectives, it could be refined the following year. No longer! You must deploy plans in a range of "rightness" or your organization may never have the opportunity to correct its course. In the past, creativity, a necessary characteristic of sales success, was sufficient to allow you to operate in a world of "smoke and mirrors." You were never called upon to explain specifically what you did to close a successful sale or what you failed to do when a sale was lost. As long as the activities and results were perceived as being right, you were left alone.

No longer! Those wagon pullers want to know *what* you plan on doing to be successful, *why* you are doing it, and *when* you plan on doing it. The rest of the organization has too much riding on your success not to be obsessively curious.

This book is being written to meet the needs of both the new sales manager and the experienced sales manager who has been in the position long enough to know the gravity of the function. It is based on the concept that the sales management role is not that of a superstar salesperson, but one of an integral member of the organizational leadership team. As such, you must now think like a manager, plan like a manager, prepare like a manager, and produce like a manager.

The sections of this book deal with the three essential tasks of great sales managers. The first part centers on the concept and associated activities of *planning*. In our urgency to meet objectives, we often fail to plan effectively. As Socrates revealed to us, never accept what is believed as absolute fact. Question long-held beliefs and try to understand what you really know, need to know more about, and don't know at all. It is no longer enough to go out and spend more time in the field coaching your sales team members.

You must first have a plan that links and integrates well with the rest of the organization.

The second part of the book centers on *preparing* for success. This is not just a state of mind. It is defining and gathering the resources (people, time, tools, and money) necessary to implement your plan. In today's heavily siloed world of organizational design and measurement, the cross-organizational functionality needed for sales success may be completely dependent on how well you prepare the rest of the organization for participation in your plan.

The last section concentrates on *producing*. This is the world that most sales managers feel comfortable in because it utilizes their past sales experience. They therefore often spend a disproportionate amount of time concentrating solely on this aspect of the role, and the result is that their management role suffers. But now that you have a plan, and all the necessary resources are in place to deliver on the plan, you must ask yourself if you have the skills to deploy, measure, and adjust your plan to meet organizational objectives for today and tomorrow.

Although this book is comprehensive, it is by no means the final knowledge you need to be successful. Always be curious about what is over the next hill, and always search for new knowledge that will make you a great sales manager.

There are a lot of wagon pullers counting on you.

PART 1

Planning

CHAPTER 1

The Changing World of Sales Management

Don't fight forces; use them.

—FULLER SHELTER (1032 A.D.)

WHAT A WORLD OF SHIFTING BUSINESS CURRENTS we live in! How can you be expected to meet your sales management goals when the tides of change have become a constant condition? Sometimes these tides move in steadily, and other times they surprise us as they suddenly surge up from unknown waters. For some reason, though, they never seem to pause and rest. When these tides of change do occur, it can often be a challenge just to keep from getting swept away by their momentum. It may be hard to visualize their direction or predict where they will carry you and your team, even for a transient period. You hope, with a sense of desperation, that the tide is moving predictably toward a new reality, but that may not be the case. All this uncertainty has placed a new burden on sales managers. We can resist these forces of change or we can leverage them for greater gain. But we first have to know where they are and where they are going.

One of the first driving forces of change is technology. Not very long ago, your customers knew about the products or services your organization offered through trade shows, promotions, or personal contacts with sales professionals. Now, however, technology has given customers the ability to search out providers from anywhere on the globe. With such an enlarged supplier pool, customers are demanding multiple channels of access to your corporation and multiple tiers of support. This has led to vendor reduction plans, strategic supplier alliances, and meet-me-in-the-middle selection processes. Customers want to know less about the features and functions of your offering and more about what your entire organization can do to solve their perceived business problems.

The next driving force is the pace of business. It has sped up so quickly that there is little, if any, time to rest on your laurels. A new idea or a new approach to your customer base quickly becomes outdated by the changing demands of the addressable marketplace. If you can't, or won't, meet the changing expectations of those who buy from you, they will switch to another provider of similar value before you know what's happening. This switchability means that companies and organizations must be in a state of continual reinvention just to stay even.

You can also add in such factors as globalization, evolving competition that looks very different from traditional competitors, shifting lifestyles and demographics, increasing mobility of employees and customers, mass customization and markets of one, addressable markets that are getting segmented and fragmented, etc. And let's not forget the migration to virtual or home-office-based selling.

While all this has been occurring, changes in the economy, along with environmental realities, have led organizations to rethink their bureaucratic structure and start paring away at perceived excesses. The result has been the elimination of many layers of management that were considered "translation layers." These critical personnel spent the majority of their time messaging information coming to them from above or below and translating the language into a format that would allow it to be understood by those next in line to receive it. The result of the elimination of these layers has been a flattening of the pyramid model for most businesses. Many large corporations went from as many as sixteen layers of management down to four or five. But without these translation layers, the surviving managers have been called upon to fill the communications or analysis vacuum and do the translations themselves—*sometimes in functional areas of the business they knew little or nothing about.*

The end result is that today's sales managers spend less time improving the selling skills of their salespeople or becoming personally involved in the sales process than they did in the past. Today, the effective sales manager is the one who thinks and acts like a member of the organization's management team. He or she provides critical situational realities to strategists and decision makers while structuring the organization's requirements into a format that will be adaptable by those at the point of customer interface.

To meet this challenge, the effective sales manager must competently assume many roles and, at times, even think up new ones that will lead to greater success. Past personal sales success is of less importance to the organization than the ability to analyze, conceptualize, and strategize. The sales manager of today must understand the changing marketplace, the competition, the general business environment, suppliers, unique characteristics of all team members, cross-organizational support mechanisms, and, most important, the mission and vision of the organization as set out by the leadership team. In other words, to be a successful sales manager, you must be "the smartest kid on the block."

So let's find out what it is that will make us smart.

What's Expected of You?

What a sense of personal accomplishment you must feel, having been chosen to lead a sales team. All those years of hard work, long hours, and extracurricular activities have paid off in career advancement, greater financial rewards, and increased power to influence decisions and directions. In all likelihood you have been selected not simply because of your sales skills, although they might have played an important part. In fact, it was most likely that you stood out to the leadership team because of your ability to make sound decisions that were in alignment with the goals of the greater organization. But what does that mean when you attempt to define the expectations that management has of you in the new role?

In most cases, management would like to see you grow the revenue. That's pretty much a given. But what else? Your organization's leaders probably would like to see you achieve some additional goals besides increased sales. Some other expectations might be:

- Increased profitability per sale

- Increased sophistication of the organization's sales professionals

- Shortened sales cycles

- Improved forecasting and trend analysis

- Expanded geographic markets

- Deeper or broader market penetration

- Client relationship building

- Expanded brand recognition

- Reduction of perceived sales chaos

- Goals and vision alignment

- Long-range planning for stability

- Market interpretation

- Dealing with problem personnel

- Cross-organizational partnering

- Improved competitiveness

- What else?

Knowing the Business Realities: Situational Analysis

Situational analysis is simply what it says: analyzing the situation. Before leaping into any action, the sales manager *must* analyze the business realities to determine what the best action would be. Additionally, after the action has been completed, another analysis must be done to determine the impact of the action on all concerned stakeholders and what, if any, further action must be taken.

What situations do you as a sales manager need to collect data on and analyze? Here are a few:

- Your industry

- Your corporation or organization

- Your unit, subsidiary, strategic business unit, division, etc.

- Your sales team

- Your sales individuals

- Your products and/or services

- Your distribution channels

- Your marketing department

- The cross-organizational resources required to meet your objectives

- Your addressable market(s) and its industry

- The targeted markets of your primary addressable customers

- Your primary competitors

- The primary competitors of your primary customers

- The general environment (the context in which all business must operate)

Perhaps the simplest and most effective tool for analyzing the business realities is the **S.W.O.T.** The letters stand for **S**trengths, **W**eaknesses, **O**pportunities, and **T**hreats. This approach provides clarity, albeit not perfect clarity, to many of the key realities around which you build your plans.

You cannot make a sales management decision without knowing these realities. In addition, the answers are not carved in stone, but fluid and continuously changing. As you are going through change, so are your customers, competitors, suppliers, and the general environment. Plan to review regularly and make adjustments based on changed or new information.

Let's take a look at a few of the most important **S.W.O.T.**s:

- Your organization or unit/division/subsidiary (any or all)

- Your sales team

- Your products and/or services

- Your primary competitor

- Your primary customer(s) or addressable market (your choice)

Description of S.W.O.T. letters:

S: Strengths of whatever you are reviewing. This is internal to the target being analyzed. It tends to be controllable and focuses on the current or present situation. Here and now, what is strong about the target? Does it have a large and loyal customer base? Are its finances good? Perhaps the company has a copyright or technology that gives it strength.

W: Weaknesses of whatever you are reviewing. This is also internal to the target being analyzed. It tends to be controllable and current, too. An example here might be that the company has a poor distribution model, aging product portfolio, or lack of brand identity.

O: Opportunities consider what might occur in the future for the target of your analysis to gain greater success, particularly if it fixes its weaknesses and leverages its strengths. This is external, less controllable, and future-focused, and might include global expansion, brand dominance, and acquisition of competitors or desired niche product providers that could expand the overall product portfolio. Remember, the company can't achieve these conditions unless it corrects its weaknesses.

T: Threats to this target's current and future success, particularly if it does not fix its weaknesses and leverage its strengths. This, too, is external, less controllable, and future-focused. Here we find such undesirable situations as hostile takeovers, bankruptcies, and loss of market share.

Note: Approach this analysis as if you were an outside consultant. Be independent in your thinking, and try not to link any of the states or conditions to any other business or conditional event. If you are reviewing your own company or sales team, *do not* complete the S.W.O.T. as you compare to other competitors. Why? Because you could easily become self-satisfied that you are better than a competitor, but in the customer's eyes, you are both failing. In other words, you end up measuring the target against the wrong benchmark. Complete your S.W.O.T. on an individual evaluation only!

S.W.O.T. Example

Your Primary Customer or Addressable Market

Strengths

- Product portfolio
- Cash reserves
- Management team
- Stable, long-term reputation
- Strong brand identity
- Defined market position perception
- Etc.

Weaknesses

- Aging customer base
- Old technology
- Fragmented distribution network
- Perceived poor customer service
- Decreasing margins
- Global infrastructure
- Etc.

Opportunities

- Diversified product line
- New acquisitions
- Newer, younger markets
- International markets
- Strategic alliances
- Pull-through sales by customer service
- Etc.

Threats

- Market elimination
- Competition with newer technology
- Zero margins due to too many competitors
- International competitors with low labor costs.
- Etc.

To add value to your S.W.O.T.s, circle items on the lists of your **Weaknesses** and **Threats** on the right. This is where you'll need to concentrate your plan.

Customer Values Benchmarking

To continue your never-ending exploration of the business realities, you must now apply some of the results of your S.W.O.T. Please do not think this is the only method you need to apply. Work closely with the members of your marketing department to integrate their *macro* view of the market with your sales-oriented *micro* view of the customers. Marketing may be deploying surveys, focus groups, consultants, market research, and other analysis tools to mine for critical information you need to be successful. The marketing staff members can be your best partners.

Let's take a look at the last S.W.O.T. you completed, the one called "Your Primary Customer(s) or Addressable Market." If you have a small number of very large, important customers, you probably did the primary customer choice. If you have many smaller customers, you probably chose the addressable market option. Either way, let's take a look at the Weaknesses and Threats that you've circled in red. This is what the decision maker's mind is locked onto!

Your target customer or market is focused on solving its weaknesses so the threats diminish. This is the very future of the organization and of people's careers. Remember, your customers are less concerned with how great your products or services are than with what you can do to solve their business problems. In other words, they want help fixing the things in your red circle.

Until you, as the sales manager, understand how to capture the mindset of your marketplace, you cannot convey this information to your leadership or construct a viable and competitive plan of action.

When you understand the mind of your market, you can benchmark your organization's competencies against those of your primary competitors in the areas that are most important to your customers. This allows you to determine specific actions you must take in a prioritized manner.

Let's take a look at how you can compare your previous results with the issues that are most important to the customers.

Step 1: Based on the last S.W.O.T. you did, and looking specifically at the *Weaknesses* and *Threats,* what do you think your addressable market or primary customer(s) would value most from a supplier/partner? Remember, do not think in terms of your products or services. That comes later. Imagine from the customer's perspective what business solutions he would need and want to correct his greatest challenges. List even those that you know your organization can't, or won't, provide.

Step 2: Now let's do a little benchmarking. How does your organization stack up in supporting these most important issues to your most important customers (+ or −)? Remember, don't rate yourself in comparison to a competitor. If you do, you may become satisfied with your competitive position when the customer is not happy with either (or all) of you. Simply, how do you rate on these issues? It might look like this:

Example

Weakness: Lack of integrated technology

Threats: Loss of market share to Internet-based competitors

Solution: Web-based product ordering system for access by their key clients.

What is needed to fix this weakness?	Rate your organization	Rate your primary competitor(s)
Technology-literate vendors	+/−	+/−
Shared research	+/−	+/−
Technology education forums	+/−	+/−
Etc.		
What is needed to counter this threat?		
Creation of a Web site	+/−	+/−
New market position	+/−	+/−
Global alliances	+/−	+/−
Etc.		

Developing Critical Objectives

Your analysis may not be perfect, but you certainly can now begin to define the most important *critical objectives* that you, as the sales manager, must address to be successful. Try to relate your customer's solutions to sales behaviors. For example, your results may have shown that you are deficient in meeting the needs of your customer's challenges on one or more of the following:

- General response time

- New or existing product development

- Sales professionalism

- Industry, product, services, or applications knowledge

- Technology interchange

- Safety or quality

- Pricing or terms and conditions

- Packaging or delivery

- Co-marketing support

- Distribution model

- Value-added resources

- Technology transfer

- Integration capabilities

- What else can you think of?

As we discussed at the beginning of this chapter, the world of sales management has changed. You must now address all of the above factors and address them in a manner that will allow you to prioritize your actions based on the issues that will have the greatest impact on sales and organizational success.

Based on what you have determined is most important to your targeted customer base and comparing your performance against your primary competitor(s), what objectives must you set for your organization, yourself, and your sales team to achieve superior results? Remember, you are now a part of the management team, and it is your responsibility to identify what needs to be fixed and to convey a plan of action in a prioritized management form of communications. No whining and no vague complaints. You need to present clear, concise, and measurable actions that have to be taken based on situational realities.

Chapter Summary

In this first chapter, we discussed the changing world of sales management and what some of the forces were behind this evolution. Additionally, we began to explore how these changes might be leading to a different set of management expectations for you and your sales team.

Next we looked at some of the business realities and concentrated on the S.W.O.T. as an excellent tool for capturing many of the most important issues for your company, your department, your competitors, and your customers. Based on the results of this tool, we narrowed down the issues that were most important to your customers and how you *and* your competitors benchmarked against them.

Finally, you were able to develop a set of critical objectives that will become the foundation for your strategic sales plan. Now you can begin additional planning, preparing, and producing activities based on your plan of action.

CHAPTER 2

Planning for Today *and* Tomorrow

First say to yourself what you would be;
and then do what you have to do.

—EPICTETUS
Discourses, Book 3, Chapter 23

WITHOUT A PLAN, YOU ARE LEFT WITH ONLY A vague concept of past tactics, a desire to do better, and uneasiness about your ability to succeed. Lacking a plan, you have no definable goals or objectives, no means of evaluating progress, and no ability to measure your advancements against your team's potential or against those with whom you are competing.

The Value of Planning

Imagine an Olympic sailor positioning the sailboat in the water wherever she or he feels like it. Continue to imagine the sailor dashing off in any old direction, regardless of the starting time, position, buoy placement, crosswinds or currents, or even where the finish line might be found. This mess could, and probably would, result in very little likelihood of winning. Truth be told, a competitor like this might not even be asked back to compete in future races. Ask yourself: Do you wish to compete in future races?

A sales manager's primary function is to collect all available information, determine the relative value of the data, and then develop and deploy a well-thought-out plan for achieving the results that will best support the organizational or corporate goal(s). With well-thought-out plans, you will be able to count on internal support, external supplier and partner support, management support, cross-organizational support, sales team support, and even the support of your key customers or target markets.

A Snapshot of Today

One of the greatest challenges for a sales manager to overcome is the temptation to construct plans based solely on egocentric ambition or antiquated historical data. Yes, it is true that if you are unaware of history's mistakes, you are doomed to repeat them. But it is even more important to understand the current changes or trends unfolding across the venue in which you are striving to succeed.

The starting point is to construct a clear image of "today." Later you will put these images into motion through trend analysis, but for now, let's just think about the current environment. There are several contributing perspectives you could review, but let's focus on the following:

■ *Technology (Hardware and/or Software).* The accelerating evolution of technology is placing a great deal of stress on business planning for two reasons. First, technology is expensive, so it's of great concern to all as to how long any selected generation of technology will be applicable before it becomes out of date. Second, an effective planner attempts to predict future directions, but that's amazingly difficult to do when one tries to picture a technology that hasn't been invented yet and lacks standards that will align the field of potential providers. One only has to think about the history of Beta versus VHS, the current battles over wireless and voice recognition models, or (perhaps) the coming standards setting requirements of quantum computing, hologram imaging, and implanted proximity biochips to understand why decision makers are so concerned.

■ *Globalization.* The world is not actually getting smaller, but it sure seems that way. Just turn your laptop computer over and look at all the countries that have contributed to its design, construction, and approval. The natural contributors that come to mind might include China, Japan, or Taiwan. But take a closer look. In addition to those countries, you might be surprised to see Turkey, Malaysia, Singapore, Israel, Argentina, Croatia, India, Cyprus, Lithuania, Latvia, the Philippines, or Slovenia. We have practiced international trade for thousands of years, but it has taken technology to allow a true, real-time global economy to function. That presents two challenges for the sales manager/planner. First, you must now prepare to compete against new global players who come into your home market, often from a well-protected home market of their own that gives them some economic advantage. This is challenging in that you often do not know enough about them to create an effective countercompetitive strategy. Second, your own domestic customers are going global, and they expect you to support them, in some manner, around the world. Going global may sound exciting, but be careful what you wish for—you just might get it. Going global can be a lot more challenging than most organizations believe.

■ *Competition.* In the past, you probably knew a great deal about the competition because your competitors lived in the same "neighborhood" as you did. In those smaller, geographically contiguous markets, our rivals often looked, walked, and talked like you. But that has all changed as the result of the growth of technology and globalization. You now find yourselves competing against virtual rivals that pop up out of nowhere and present an impressive face, via a Web site, to the customers you had thought were your most protected. Your virtual rivals may look as big as IBM, but are actually just three people working out of a garage in Brazil. Thanks to the Internet and FedEx, they can provide offerings to customers anywhere in the world overnight—just like us (maybe)!

So what do you know about them? Are they partially owned by a foreign government or considered a protected national treasure, making it very hard, in either case, to collect competitive information about them? How important is their competing product to their overall business? How do they view themselves, and how do they make decisions? What is their competing cost? Their structure and distribution model? How do they view us? To put it in terms you've already discussed, what's their S.W.O.T.?

■ *Customers.* About 100 years ago, Henry Ford deployed the concept of *mass production.* I'm sure he wasn't really the first, but he certainly got credit for it in the new industrial age that was blossoming at the time. Up until Mr. Ford's time, automobiles were the playthings of the rich, who were the only ones who could afford them. In being able to apply the golden age of manufacturing to the benefit of the average consumer, Ford and his peers required absolute consistency in processes to deliver the exciting new offerings at a reasonable price. He best exemplified the need by stating that buyers could have any color Ford they wanted as long as it was black. He was in control!

As America grew, and changed, people like Henry Ford found it harder and harder to control the requirements of a consumer who was moving out of the cities and into the pasture lands—better known as the suburbs. Intermediaries were needed to cover this broader, more distributed marketplace. Ford deployed dealers. Others chose to sell through retailers, wholesalers, and distributors. Subtly, the power shifted in the supply chain from the manufacturers to the retailers. Consumers began to care more about where they bought it than about who manufactured it. They wanted convenience in purchasing, and outlets like Sears, Graybar, and, later, Home Depot gained the upper hand. As soon as these intermediaries recognized their new power, they demanded that the manufacturers design and create the products the way they wanted to sell them or they would go to a no-name producer to make them the way they wanted. Americans moved away from mass production and toward *mass customization*. They even went so far as to demand their own branded labels on products produced by others (e.g., Albertsons private labels, Gap, and CVS).

Over the last decade, though, the shift has occurred again.

Now, thanks to technology and globalization, consumers are no longer bound by the offerings of outlets within their geographic area. If prospective buyers don't see their pet's favorite rice and lamb stew at a local pet-food store, they can go online and find someone in the world who does have what they want. And, thanks again to overnight shipping, they can have it in their homes or offices the next day. With this newfound power, consumers are telling the world they no longer want to be treated like everyone else; they want to be sold to in a manner that is unique to them. Not like their relatives and not like their neighbors. They are now demanding that they be treated as a *market of one*. The problem for a planner is to understand how that market of one views value and how it goes about making purchase decisions.

■ *Demographics.* It is nearly impossible for a business to integrate the advantages of mass production, the variations of mass customization, and the diversity of markets of one into a competitive sales strategy. Somehow you have to find enough markets of one, even if they are not contiguously located, to take advantage of state-of-the-art production techniques. The problem is that old models of market demographics are based on mass customization models and can't account for the diversity within a group or category. For example, the fastest growing demographic group (and largest minority) in the United States is a grouping entitled "Hispanic." In the past, businesses produced Hispanic-oriented advertising to cover this targeted market. But ask yourself about the similarities and differences among Hispanics born and raised in Tucson, those born and raised in Miami, and those born and raised in Brooklyn. The differences between them need to be explored as much as their similarities. In addition to cultures, you must consider gender, age, education, hobbies, interests, professions, and so much more.

What do you really know about your customers? How do they make decisions? What knowledge must they have to make a decision in your favor? Values, belief systems, and judgment paradigms are not the exclusive realm of the end consumer; they are well entrenched in corporate offices, too.

■ *Lifestyles.* Once you decide what your perfect customers look like, you need to recognize the changes that are going on in lifestyles, not just in the United States, but around the world. Of course, people are more mobile and distributed. That reality may have already sunk in as you manage a virtual home office salesperson in another time zone. But think about this lifestyle change: people are living longer. The question that presents itself to us is, what part of life are you extending? Certainly not childhood or adolescence or even early adulthood. Old age has certainly been extended, but there seems to be another focus these days. When I was a child, you retired at age 65 because you were burnt out. By 70, you were in a retirement or convalescent home because you could no longer care for yourself. Not very good golden years, were they? One of the greatest changes in lifestyles these days is the expansion of the upper-middle-age bracket. How many sixty-five- or seventy-year-olds do you still find actively contributing to an organization or even starting their own new business? A whole lot of them! But if that is the current trend, how will it impact your sales plan? Also a whole lot!

■ *Psychographics (Consumer Sentiment).* There are a lot of variations around this terminology, but I like to consider it the *mood of the consumer.* How consumers feel about "things" is extremely important to the supply chain. If they aren't happy, in most cases they aren't spending money. Some experts contend that there are only two groups that are not affected by the end consumer—the military and the government. I believe that those two groups are also affected because politicians know consumers vote with their emotional feelings about issues they perceive as affecting them, so they had better manage spending in line with the majority of consumer expectations.

■ *Firmographics (Business Sentiment).* Another trend to consider is that of the mood of business, or more correctly, of the business leadership. Often times, this mood is out of alignment with the mood of the consumer mentioned previously. For example, when the economic bubble began to burst toward the end of the twentieth century, consumers thought it was a momentary snag and kept on spending. Business leaders—at least the intelligent ones—knew immediately that they were in trouble. They had built an organizational or corporate infrastructure designed to support the needs of the bubble economy. When the bubble burst, businesses were too big and too expensive to run in the lean and mean economy. What followed were layoffs, restructurings, and bankruptcies (in addition to the broken promises made to employees and shareholders). The businesses you sell to or through will not buy or buy more until their sentiment improves and is once again in alignment with consumer sentiment.

■ *Economy.* Quick, which economy was better? The bubble economy of the 1990s or the bottomed-out economy of the early 2000s? Not sure? Neither am I. As this book is being written, the current state of the economy is tough. There does seem to be a turnaround on the horizon, but if it comes, it will be slow due to a lack of trust generated from so many false promises by pseudoexperts espousing unethical, forged financial forecasts. The bubble economy might have appeared to be better, but it was doomed to failure because of poor attention to detail, including bad or nonexistent business plans.

As a sales manager, either way you look at it, it is challenging to figure out where the current trend in the economy is going and what it might mean to your strategic sales plans.

■ *Regulatory Practices.* No matter what your political leanings are, you seem to be living in an increasingly regulated world. From consumers through manufacturers, every day brings new guidelines, regulations, and standards. To top if off, thanks to globalization, you may find your products, market approach, or personnel being regulated by governments or industry committees from halfway around the world. Just look at the raging controversy over genetically modified foods or the trade barrier wars at the World Trade Organization.

■ *Business Practices.* Based on what you have just reviewed, there are a lot of pressures on the marketplace that you are trying to sell into. There are also pressures on the company you work for, your suppliers, your partners, your distributors, your competitors, and your customers. As these pressures, from technological to regulatory, have evolved, businesses have attempted to address the changes with adaptations to the way they practice their profession. You now have such things as laptop and desktop computers, pooled resource networks, personal digital assistants, e-mail, voice mail, wireless links, global pagers and walkie-talkies, tele-conferences, contract employees, and virtual or home offices. The struggle has been to incorporate these new practices into traditional practices. Unfortunately, most businesses have re-sponded to this practice change by relying more on activity-based measurements than on performance measurements.

Scenario and Simulation Planning

Once you have estimated where a contributor to sales suc-cess currently is, you must now put that contributor in mo-tion. Certainly snapshots are valuable, but they don't tell you where the contributor has been or where it is going. Consider psychographics. To say that the mood of the consumer is slightly "negative" about the economy doesn't help much. Only by looking at previous data and trending out the changes can you determine whether this current mood is a growing negativity or an improvement in attitude.

Once you have a history-to-present trend for any contributor, you can project that trend out into the future. You can also incorporate future alternative events that may have an im-pact on your plans. There are two excellent, and easy to apply, trend projection techniques that you can use with your sales team. Remember, the more diverse the input, the better the results.

Scenario Planning

This tool is based on the concept that there is more than one possible future. A skilled planner must uncover the most likely scenarios and find the environmental indicators that announce which one seems to be the unfolding future. Start by having your diverse planning team brainstorm current trends and develop a reasonably clear picture of a future business environment about five years out. Next, have the team identify several significant indicators that demonstrate that the environment is truly moving in the imagined direction.

Example

Scenario 1: Five years from now, the business environment will be stronger than today, with very large and very small competitors driving the markets based on control and management of information that support a focus on a "market-of-one" approach.

Indicators for Scenario 1: Sustained improvement of major economic indicators, reduction of medium-size businesses, increase in venture capital funded start-ups, focus on smaller and smaller market segments, increase in data mining and manipulation software, increased electronic customer interface channels based on individual preferences, blurring of the distinction between sales and marketing organizations due to the need for greater "customer intimacy."

Once your team has created a single vision for the future and defined some of the indicators that demonstrate that your future world is truly unfolding, you've only completed part of the exercise. You must now place those indicators in logical sequence and create a timeline map for the five-year period.

Don't relax too soon. You now need to create three to four alternative, yet realistic and attainable, futures. They need to be different from your first ones, and each will have its own set of indicators.

Example

Scenario 2: Five years from now, the business environment will be weaker and more chaotic than today, with major industries moving to offshore locations resulting in loss of intellectual capabilities and technological leadership.

Indicators for Scenario 2: No improvement in the major economic indicators, increasing loss of service industry jobs, increase in global competition, new technology standards being driven and set by countries such as China and India, decline in foreign-born student enrollment in American colleges, and shrinkage of previous industry leaders based in the United States.

The final result is that you can now begin to construct your plans around a trended future, know what indicators to watch for, and be prepared when different events require you to alter your plans.

Simulation Planning

This form of "future" trending is somewhat similar to the scenario process, but it segments out the primary drivers for analysis before combining them for some specific period in the future. Let's start by taking another look at your eleven identified drivers that impact sales success:

1. Technology (hardware and/or software)

2. Globalization

3. Competition

4. Customers

5. Demographics

6. Lifestyles

7. Psychographics (consumer sentiment)

8. Firmographics (business sentiment)

9. Economy

10. Regulatory practices

11. Business practices

Break your planning group into eleven individual teams with each one focusing on only one of the drivers listed above. It is best to select members for a particular team who are subject matter experts in the field. For example, bring some IT folks into your session to concentrate on technology or some government affairs personnel to focus on regulatory practices.

Separate the groups into different planning locations and ask each to determine where their driver has been, where it is currently, and (if the trend continues) where it might most likely be in five years.

Finally, bring the teams back together again and overlay the drivers to create a vision of some specific time in the future. You and your team will be amazed at how clear an image develops. The pace of change is speeding up to the point where the future will not be a bigger, faster, shinier version of today.

Although you are not fortune-tellers, you must try to grasp a view of tomorrow to do better planning today.

Determining Prioritized Corporate Objectives

Many sales managers become so entrapped in their own team's goals that they forget that the primary objective of a sales department is to help the overall organization meet its goals. You serve a specific purpose: to sell the company's products or services through strong and effective customer interactions. But you are only one piece of the overall puzzle, and you need to recognize the larger objectives of your organization.

Often sales managers and their sales team members talk about the company only wanting more sales or revenue. In fact, increased sales are often only one component of some larger objectives of the organization. What is your organization's vision of what would be gained from increased sales? Let's look at a few examples:

- Profitability improvement

- Increased shareholder value

- Strengthening brand identity

- Increased geographic coverage

- New market-segment expansion

- Deterrent to growing competition

- Acquisitions

- Increased professionalism

- Broadening product or service lines

- What else?

Corporate objectives are usually much clearer than you think. Consider developing a few questions you might like to ask your leadership. Here are a few ideas:

- What are the greatest opportunities in the organization's future?

- What are the greatest challenges to the organization's future?

- Who is creating long-term strategic plans for the organization? (This can be, and probably is, more than one person.)

- What are their stated short- and long-term objectives?

- How could their objectives be prioritized?

- What do they see as the sales organization's contribution to these objectives? (Make sure they are as specific as possible.)

Spend time with your senior management and executives to get answers to these questions. Remember, you are looking for answers pertaining to the organization as a whole. It will be your job to narrow the required action down to a sales plan. Approach such a discovery interview just as you did when you were out selling. Listen for the emotions and intent behind the words, not just the words themselves.

Clarifying Short-Term, Intermediate, and Long-Term Goals

What you have just discovered are the prioritized goals of your organization as a whole. You have also defined what your team's contribution to the attainment of these goals might and should be. You must now develop some short-term, intermediate, and long-term goals for your sales team.

Short-term goals are defined as those results that can be achieved in twelve months or less. They are often stated as your team's sales quotas, but they are also there to support your organization's yearly objectives, as created and viewed by the leadership, the investors and, of course, the capital markets or capital markets community. They generate immediate cash flow for the company that will, hopefully, exceed expenditures and justify your organization's approach to contributing to the strategic plan. Short-term goals can usually be achieved with existing resources with only minor modifications to personnel, products, support, or the customer base.

Many sales managers find themselves in difficulty because they focus only on longer-term objectives for their team. If you look closely at the first items on the list of your organization's prioritized goals for the organization as a whole, you will recognize that there are some that must be achieved right away. They may be:

- Increased sales revenue

- Increased profitability or margin on the average sale

- Improved order entry quality to reduce returns

- Costs control and/or staff reductions

- New product or service acceptance by the targeted market

- New geographic expansion

- What else? (Must be attainable in under twelve months)

Long-term goals are usually defined as those results that can be achieved only over a longer period of time, say five to seven years. They tend to be linked with the long-term vision of the organization as a whole, and several complex changes and steps must be made to attain these goals.

Some of these changes are dramatic and can cause instability to a sales organization. The best way to prevent this is to have *clear, concise,* and *measurable* pathways to achieve these long-term goals. They may be:

- New market penetration

- Strategic sales alliances

- Cross-organizational team selling

- Complete change of customer's brand perception

- What else? (Must require a period of time to attain)

Intermediate goals are those that fall somewhere between the short- and long-term goals, usually around three years. They could be called milestones because they are often used to sustain support for the long-term goals. Nothing succeeds like success, and these goals are used to persuade senior management and executives that your ideas and reasoning are sound and that significant advances toward your long-term goals are being made. They *must* link the short- and long-term goals, and they might include such areas as:

- Sales competency training curriculums

- Sustained sales growth

- New electronic connectivity platforms

- What else? (Must require a period of time to attain)

Are they S.M.A.R.T. Goals?
Specific,
Measurable,
Attainable,
Relevant, and
Time Framed

Creating Directional Statements for Your Sales Team

Do you know where you need to take your team in the near and long-term future? If called upon, could you easily and clearly communicate these goals to any and all interested parties? Let's take a look at some sales management tools to do just that.

Mission and Vision Statements

In essence, you have just constructed the foundation of a *mission statement* and a *vision statement* for your sales organization. Surprised that you need them? You may have thought that these directional statements are only for the organization as a whole. The truth is, exceptionally well-run companies have a mission statement and a vision statement for every department. There are two important considerations when constructing directional statements. First, they must be aligned from your sales organization up through the overall corporate statements. Second, they must support the coordinated long-term approach to a vision of success. Let's take a look at these two powerful statements.

Mission Statement

A *mission statement* is intended to reach the same audience as the short-term goals. It should influence your senior management and executives, all required immediate support organizations, investors, and the capital markets community. One of the simplest ways of creating a mission statement is to ask the following question:

Being the best you can be, with the resources you currently have available, how would you like your sales team to be described?

Notice that this does not ask for a description of your current sales team. It asks for a description of how the team might appear after you have maximized the potential of your total resources. The answer can be a single paragraph or a sentence with bullet points. Either way, keep it simple and use clear, concise, and measurable terms.

Vision Statement

A *vision statement* is a directional statement intended to create a motivational environment by giving the personnel a view of the future that they can enthusiastically support. Like a good sales presentation, the vision statement must meet both the wants and the needs of your sales team and all supporting departments. In other words, it must reach the *mind* and the *heart*—particularly in this day of fragile corporate–employee relationships.

Although there are many ways to look at this directional statement, a good way to arrive at a vision statement might simply be to ask:

Making changes into the future, how would you like your sales team to be described at some definable future date?

Notice, here we are talking about making *changes*. Not simply living with what we have or making minor modifications to our current sales team, but making changes. The vision statement has no destination point; it is considered a direction or pathway. You always want to be moving toward a future vision. This must also align well both with the long-term goals of your sales team and with the overall vision for the organization as a whole. Once again, keep it simple and use clear and concise words, not interpretative words. You shouldn't have to explain or translate it.

Determining Resource Requirements and Availability

You have now completed some key documents involved in successful sales force planning. So far, you have:

- Developed a snapshot of the current environment

- Applied trend analysis to your snapshot to give you a vision of the future

- Determined prioritized corporate objectives

- Clarified short-term, intermediate, and long-term goals

- Created directional statements for your sales team

Identifying Key Players and Their Motivators

Now you are getting down to the wire in planning documentations. The next step is to realize that you can't achieve all these wonderful goals by yourself or with only your sales team. You will need internal and external resources, and you will need to "name names." For example, if you plan to increase customer acceptance of new products or services, you might need the following:

Product management: To change pricing strategy

Advertising: To provide effective push-pull marketing

Finance: To develop some long-term, low-interest financing

Order processing: To expedite orders for this product

Customer service: To handle inquiries and service calls more effectively

But knowing which department to call upon will not lead to goal success. You will need to establish a relationship with key individuals within the department to gain their support. Consider specifically whom you might need now and in the future. This can often be more than one individual or function. For example, you may need an outbound telemarketing representative. But if you borrow this person from his or her current assignment, you'll be impacting the measurements placed on that person and department by his or her manager. Always spend time getting to know the evaluators of the person or function you need. Remember, when you make even a minor modification, you are altering an entire web of linkages.

After you've identified the departments and key players, you need to discover what it is that drives their performance. In most cases, it will be the measurements with which they are evaluated at the end of the year. If you are to gain their total support, you must be willing to support their efforts, too.

Rechecking Prioritized Corporate Objectives

One final planning note. Your organization is always changing. The environment changes, the leadership changes, the customer base changes, the technology changes, and the needs of investors change. As you have seen in the scenario planning discussion earlier, the future may turn out to be very different than you had planned.

Schedule time to regularly recheck your short-term, intermediate, and long-term goals to assure that they are in complete alignment with ever changing business realities. Watch for the indicators that will tell you when a shift in direction is taking place and adjust accordingly. The last thing you want to do is find yourself traveling down the wrong path.

Key Rechecks

- Annual reports

- Quarterly reports

- Press releases

- Internal and external speeches by key individuals

- Outside evaluators (financial community and auditors)

- Changes in organizational mission and vision statements

- Your managers

- Your leaders

- Other department heads

Chapter Summary

In this chapter, we talked about the value of planning for both short- and long-term goals. Without a solid plan, you cannot set directions, establish and manage to measurements, or recognize when the situation is changing. Your plan may not always be exactly right, but without it you have nothing with which to benchmark your progress.

You start with giving serious thought to current trends, and then through scenario or simulation planning, project these trends into the future to estimate future requirements.

Equally important is the need to clarify organizational objectives before you set your own sales department goals. Once you have done that, an effective sales manager sets short-term goals to meet immediate needs of the organization, long-term goals to lead to future success, and intermediate goals to measure success. This important direction is often captured in a strong mission and vision statement.

The final step in planning is to determine resource requirements to help you meet your goals: Decide which key players need to be engaged, recognize what their motivation might be to help you be successful, and continually recheck the corporate goals to do the necessary fine-tuning of your plans.

CHAPTER 3

Crafting the Professional Sales Force

Whatever is worth doing at all is worth doing well.

—LORD CHESTERFIELD
Letters to His Son, March 10, 1746

NOW THAT YOU HAVE DETERMINED YOUR objectives for today and tomorrow, the time has come to construct a sales force model. You may have already inherited a team of professionals, but following these steps from beginning to end will allow you to refine and develop personnel now and in the future.

Setting Out Your Goals

The best way to start is to put some specific measurements in place. Not just any measurements, but ones designed to specifically impact the short- and long-term goals you defined in Chapter 2. Some have called this "grounding the vision." This means taking the goals out of the sky and placing them in the realities of your current situation.

To do this, you will require a team of contributors, as shown in Figure 3-1.

Figure 3-1. Contributions to a realistic vision.

As Lewis Carroll said in *Alice in Wonderland,* if you don't care where you are going, you are sure to get there if you walk long enough. Well, maybe in Mr. Carroll's day, or in Alice's new world, you could take as long as you needed to get somewhere, but not today! Not in this rapidly changing world of technology-based global business. You just don't have that much time to reach success, so you'd better start establishing performance objectives and measurements.

Establishing Performance Objectives and Measurements

One thing to keep in mind is that you cannot do it "the same old way." That would be like trying to drive an old oversized luxury car from the 1950s today. It may be beautiful to look at and comfortable to ride in, but the quality, gas mileage, and shortage of technologies will make it useless for anything but an antique auto exhibit.

There are four areas to consider when creating or setting performance objectives. These are:

1. Needs of the business

2. Performance needs

3. Training needs

4. Work environment needs

Do you notice the sequence? The order of solutions has usually been found to work best when you follow the above sequence. Remember, the sales department is not an island unto itself. You are performing the sales function to meet some organization-wide need(s), so start with the needs of the business and progress to the needs of the work environment. As you look at any desired performance objective, construct a process improvement analysis that looks like the one in Figure 3-2.

Step 1: What Is the Current Performance Level of the Organization?

■ *How are its measurements compared to where they should be right now?* How is your overall organization performing against its stated objectives and goals? If you aren't sure, sit down with the leadership and find out.

■ *What is the current sales organization's contribution to the organization's overall current performance?* Be honest and explore this subject as you develop your performance improvement plan. Be realistic in a manner that will be relevant to all concerned. Don't deny or minimize your depart-

Figure 3-2. Linking performance to gap closure.

Operational Results   Sales Performance Results

| 1. What is the current performance level of the organization? | AS-IS → | 2. What is the current performance level of the sales department? |

Gap   *Gap*

| 3. What are the organization's performance objectives? | TO-BE → | 4. What must the sales department achieve to meet these objectives? |

| 5. What environmental factors, outside our control, are impacting sales performance results? |

ment's contribution to a shortfall in goal attainment by the company. At the same time, don't fall on a sword that is not of your creation. Be honest so that you will be perceived by all as a true member of the organization's management team.

Step 2: What Is the Current Performance Level of the Sales Department?

■ *Identification of current performance and organizational obstacles.* Now that you know what performance levels you need to have as a sales organization, take a look at where you are now. Don't generalize with such concepts as "we aren't very good" or "we don't make enough sales." Be specific. In what performance areas are you currently lacking, and by exactly how many sales are you falling short? This analysis will give you a starting point to measure success in the coming months and years.

Also, be realistic about organizational obstacles that might make it difficult to improve. Just because these challenges exist, however, does not mean you can treat them as excuses. If it were that easy, anybody could do your job. You are being paid to mitigate or find a way around the obstacles.

■ *Relative importance of all performance results.* As you look at the current performance results, identify and categorize them enough to be able to prioritize or rank them in their importance for meeting the desired performance requirements demanded by your answers to Step 1. Everyone is limited by time, money, tools, and people. Make sure that you are working on the performance standards that will have the greatest impact on the successful achievement of your goals. This works for you in two ways. First, it helps keep the entire organization supporting your plans. Second, it keeps your sales team engaged since the performance improvement that you require of them is directly linked to organizational success and is not perceived as just busy work.

■ *Current skills to perform as required.* Ask yourself specifically, what are the current skills of the sales team members (or those currently performing the sales function) in areas that have an impact on the highest priorities identified in the last question? If you have a sales team now, analyze each of them individually, not as a team. This will allow you to develop a performance improvement plan for each, rather than grouping them all together in an ill-defined initiative.

■ *Obstacles to performance.* Make sure you consider any current obstacles that need to be addressed to reach your, and the organization's, goals. Be realistic since some of them, such as current compensation models, HR-controlled benefits programs, inadequate product portfolio, insufficient supportive technology, available talent pool, decline in addressable markets, might affect your success.

■ *Skill gaps.* This point is very important. Based on your analysis of what is needed to perform at the level required to meet organization or corporate objectives and the current level that the performance is at today, what is the gap? Whether it is per sales person or per the entire team, you now have a starting point, a finish line, and a distance you have to traverse to be successful. This gap will help you set the intermediate goals and milestones of measurement to communicate to the world that you are doing a great job.

Step 3: What Are the Organization's Performance Objectives?

■ *Identification of internal business goals and challenges.* As we said in the previous chapters, a sales manager must always be focused on the organization's goals, objectives, and challenges. Make sure you have a very clear understanding of the vision for the future held by the leadership of your business, association, or organization. Don't make assumptions, have preconceived ideas, or jump to conclusions based on partial data. Sit down with your leaders and ask them specifically what performance level would they like to see the organization achieving. Not just the sales team, but the entire organization. Make sure that they discuss their views of what obstacles or challenges might lie in the way.

■ *Identification of customer goals and challenges.* Additionally, review your S.W.O.T. on the customer segment you are targeting. Consider the goals and challenges of your most important customers. More than a few successful sales managers have engaged their targeted market in the performance-setting process for their sales team.

■ *Understanding the implications of performance as viewed by both functional management and the customer.* The next action for Step 3 is to explore the way your organization's management team perceives the contribution that the sales organization can make to achieve the overall organizational objective. This is critical! You must understand their view of the role of sales. It might surprise you.

Step 4: What Must the Sales Department Achieve to Meet These Objectives?

■ *Identification of required performance results.* Now, find out your required contribution to the organization's overall goal attainment. You can't bear the whole burden on your shoulders, but as the initiating department for new orders, you do share a significant portion of the burden for organizational success. Be realistic about what sales performance levels are required of your team and don't get bogged down in the "we can't do that" mode of thinking. You can do just about anything if you address realities in your planning. Link your team's contribution to some form of performance evaluation that is *clear, concise,* and *measurable.* Clear means that any reader will be able to understand it. Concise means it is to the point without bombastic wordage. Measurable means you are able to determine the impact. It might be a specific increase in gross margins on the average sale. Or it might be an increase in cost reduction through an increase in order entry quality as measured by returned orders. It could be issues related to customer retention as measured by lost customer rate. It might even be a reduction in internal conflicts between the sales department and other organizational departments as measured by cross-organizational surveys. Remember, if you can't measure it, it doesn't belong in the performance standards.

■ *Identification of customer's required performance model.* Spend some time with your most important customers, those you can't afford to lose, and find out what they require in a sales professional that provides solutions to their business challenges. Make sure you focus on the field and hierarchal level you are selling into, such as IT management or enterprise-wide directorships, so the data will be clear about the point of interaction.

■ *Identification of senior management's required performance model.* Here we are analyzing, in partnership with our senior management, the requirements for a sales performance model. In other words, we understand from previous questions how they perceive the sales department in regard to its contribution to overall organizational success. But what departmental design or model do they require? In some organizations, the senior management or leadership demands accessibility to the sales team with some form of ability to influence daily activities. In other organizations, senior management prefers that the sales team be part of the marketing department or customer service. In others, you might have complete autonomy and independence. You can't simply shape a perfect sales model and establish performance objectives without senior management's input on a required or desired departmental model.

■ *Agreement with sales personnel for skills development actions.* Whether they are new kids out of the gate or old seasoned veterans, you now have the basis for communicating to your sales personnel a plan for improving the skills that are necessary to meet organization goals and objectives, as outlined in individual performance improvement plans. You will get a greater acceptance of the plan and an agreement by your team to being measured by the new standards of performance because they are directly linked to the goals of the organization as a whole.

■ *Agreement with senior management for skills development actions.* To ensure the support and confidence of your senior management team, as well as cross-organizational support, gain the agreement of your leadership to your specific plan of action to improve performance results. As you might be aware, leaders do not like surprises, and if they encounter any, you surely don't want them to come from your sales plan.

Step 5: What Environmental Factors Outside Your Control Are Impacting Performance Results?

■ *What is the current state of your organization?* As you step back and look at your company or association, what are the realities? I have been called in many times to work with companies that are in decline because of a lack of interest by the ownership or a disappearing target market. I've also been called in to situations where the global companies are challenged to communicate effectively in diverse cultures, where there is a demand for different approaches to success in localized markets. I don't mean that we just give up in these situations, but we must incorporate them into a plan that accounts for any realities we need to work around and through if we want to attain success.

■ *What is the current state of the business drivers we talked about in Chapters 1 and 2?* Remember the business drivers? The current, trending, and future of each must be incorporated in your sales plan if it is to have any validity.

- Technology (hardware and/or software)

- Globalization

- Competition

- Customers

- Demographics

- Lifestyles

- Psychographics (consumer sentiment)

- Firmographics (business sentiment)

- Economy

- Regulatory practices

- Business practices

Be honest and explore each of the previous questions as you develop your performance improvement plans, and as you do, ask yourself the following questions:

- How good is your business intent? Is it in complete alignment with all realities?

- What are the key business drivers mentioned previously that will have the greatest impact on success?

- What do you know about the internal environment? Do you need to know more, and where will you go to get that information?

- What do you know about the external environment? Do you need to know more, and where will you go to get that information?

Raising the Bar for Existing Sales Team Members

As you set performance standards for your team members, you must establish ones that will drive a higher and higher level of performance from your existing sales personnel. As I mentioned previously, you cannot do this as a group, but rather from the unique individuality of each person. No matter what you are creating as a new expectation, each person will be starting from a different point in his or her control and understanding of the performance skill set.

Measure where your team members are, where you want them to be, how much time is available to improve their performance skills, and what their rate of learning is. Also, develop a performance improvement plan that is based on where you want them to be both in the short term and twelve months from now.

The one key to performance improvement for existing team members is that they must recognize and understand the relevance of the performance standard to the business environment. If they don't, they will be hesitant and resistant.

Using the New Performance Standards to Hire

It can be much easier to set standards for the new hires. Add any required performance skills to a list you will be creating in the next chapter. It will make hiring much easier since you can now specifically measure all possible candidates, both internal and external, against a valuable competencies scale.

But, remember, you cannot have a performance standard for new hires that is different from the one for existing team members. This will only lead to dissatisfaction and complications in the compensation program, as well as possible legal problems for you and the company. Make sure that you are being fair to all team members.

Chapter Summary

In this chapter we discussed the need for establishing clear, reasonable performance measurements for each and every team member. Rather then being constructed arbitrarily, this is done by linking the approach to internal and external factors, gap analysis, and the overall organizational business plan. The resulting performance analysis can be used both to raise the bar for existing team members and to set equally high standards for new hires.

PART 2

Preparing

CHAPTER 4

Finding the Talent

Leave no stone unturned.

—EURIPIDES,
Heraclidae (c. 482 B.C.)

TIME AFTER TIME, IN BOTH CONSULTING AND training, I've found that one of the greatest areas of concern for most sales managers is the hiring process. This is true for the new sales manager who lacks experience and for seasoned managers who find changing demographics in the available talent pool and changing demands of the marketplace. Not only is there the challenge of locating and capturing the right candidate, but there is also a legitimate concern about the consequences to the organization, and to themselves, of hiring the wrong person.

Recruiting and Hiring Practices

In every case, sales managers have their personal strengths and weaknesses when it comes to hiring. Just like sports coaches, some are good at locating and recruiting while others shine during the interview process. Some even excel at integrating the recruit quickly into their new work environment. Some just wish anybody, other than themselves (like the human resources department), would take over the responsibility. Well, the accountability, no matter who recruits, interviews, and hires, is you! You're going to have to work with, and develop, the newly acquired salespeople, so you need to become engaged in the process as early as possible.

There are several perspectives to take into consideration when hiring, and no one perspective is of greater value than another. They must all be taken into account when initiating a hiring activity. They include, not in any particular order:

- Your needs

- The needs of your sales team

- The needs of the customers and the territory

- The needs of the organization as a whole

- The needs of the candidates

Your Needs

If you are to be successful as a sales manager, you must find someone who will mesh well with you and your objectives. If your sales team is to excel, you must find someone who will be supportive of, and not disruptive to, the team's overall performance. If you want to see rapid success from your new hires, you must find someone who can grasp the unique dynamics of each sales territory and the characteristics of the targeted marketplace. Additionally, the most productive and beneficial results will come from someone who can harmonize with other parts of your organization. Finally, as with all human interactions, you must treat the candidate with dignity and respect. Your professionalism during this hiring process will reflect on you and your organization for years to come.

The Needs of Your Sales Team

This can be an eye-opening analysis. Since every sales team is unique, think about the dynamics. Ask the following questions:

■ *Does the team function as a true team or as a collection of individuals?* This will help you determine the kind of support a new hire will receive from the existing team members, and the amount of time you will need to be engaged in training and coaching. Will you need a self-starter who is a quick learner or someone who learns best by observing and partnering with your more seasoned sales pros?

■ *Do team members work together in the same office or do they work out of virtual or home offices?* Can new hires quickly get answers to their questions, or will they have to be creative in finding solutions? Are data and knowledge easily accessible? If new hires are going to work out of a home office, how strong do they have to be in self-management, time management, and cost control?

■ *Is there a dominating individual or natural team leader on the team?* If the answer is yes, what type of personality will be required to blend with that person, and what role will that individual realistically play in the selection and development of the new hire?

■ *Will the team readily accept and help train a new member? How does the current team see the new hire?* Is there someone who might fear the new hire is going to steal away part of his territory and, therefore, income? Or does the team desperately need the new hire to decrease the stress of being overworked? Maybe someone even sees the person as a possible replacement because of an unsatisfactory management opinion.

■ *Considering the S.W.O.T. on your sales team, is there some unique competency that you would like in the new hire that would be beneficial to the other team members?* What contribution can the new hire make to the overall success of the team? Perhaps he or she has expertise in technology or graphic arts or proposal writing.

The Needs of Your Customers and the Territory

Try to make your best customers your partners in the hiring process. Ask them what characteristics they would prefer to have in a sales professional who might be calling on them. Since customers are demanding solutions, rather than products, should the new candidate possess financial analysis or strategic planning skills?

At the same time, consider the territory demands that can be placed on an individual. Is this a high "churn" territory or a stable one? Is there a lot of traveling or very little? Is the environment highly competitive? What will be the primary contact level and role at the customer's business? Is there a particular personality style that might be more successful?

The Needs of Your Organization as a Whole

As mentioned earlier, more than one sales manager has been brought down by organizational politics. Many times it is not the SM creating the trouble, but one of her sales team members. You need to spend a great deal of planning time considering the world that this new hire will operate in and what your organization will expect from him or her. No matter how great a salesperson she may turn out to be, if she can't get along with the other departments within your company, it will reflect badly on her and on you.

Ask yourself what the perceived role of sales is within your organization. Is it carrying any baggage? What will the new hire's interactions be with senior management or executives? Will they be required to work with other departments to satisfy customer needs and wants? If the answer to either question is yes, then you must consider some of the most important competencies required to work well with other senior leadership or departments across your organization.

The Needs of the Candidate

Before you move on to hiring practices, give some thought to the poor folks who are applying for your open position. Remember what it was like when you applied for a new position? Probably pretty scary. Here are some areas to be very clear about during the hiring process:

- Always let the applicant know exactly what will be expected of him or her during the process.

- Keep the applicant informed of the selection progress and of key milestone dates.

- Whether you choose the applicant or not, give feedback on your perception of his or her strengths and weaknesses.

■ Let applicants who are not selected know immediately. Don't keep them hanging on the line because you hate to give out bad news.

The professionalism of your hiring approach will reflect positively or negatively on you and your company. Strive to do it well and always be honest and ethical when interacting with candidates.

Loaded with a list of "needs" identified in the last chapter, as well as the key thoughts discussed earlier in this chapter, you are now ready to begin your search for the acquisition of the talent that will make your sales team a star performance group. Make sure you are not just working from a "gut" feeling, but from a well-developed list of criteria such as the following:

■ What is the position you would like to fill?

■ What are the top three competencies you require of this person now?

■ What additional competencies would you like to see this person develop within twelve months?

■ What additional competencies are required by the organization?

■ What additional competencies are required by the customers and the territory?

■ What additional personal attributes and financial realities are involved?

■ What are the performance objectives?

Be sure to validate your criteria with your management, your peers, your best customers, and your sales team. They will not have all the answers, but they can add valuable insights.

How to Recruit

You now have your list of requirements and a simple job description for a profile to be used during the hiring process. But where are the best candidates hiding? Well, there are several channels you can pursue to find the best sales talent. Let's take a look at a few:

Internal

- Personal references from existing sales personnel (always the best place to start)

- Human resources department

- Other departmental personnel that have shown a customer focus

- Company newsletter

- Company bulletin boards

External

- Associations

- Conferences

- Special events

- Friends

- Competitors *(Be careful!)*

- Recruiting services

- Contingency firms

- Retained agents

- Advertising

- Web sites

- Industry periodicals

- Newspapers

- Radios

One of the most important functions of an advertisement to fill an open sales position is to define the assignment in a manner that will eliminate the majority of potential applicants. In other words, as busy as you are, make sure you receive applications only from those people who are qualified to do the job successfully. For example, if the open sales position requires extensive travel that will necessitate the salesperson's being away from home 40 percent of the time, say so. If the job requires a college degree in the biological sciences, say so. If specific computer or analytical skills are required, say so. If presentation or public speaking skills are required, say so.

Interviewing "Best Practices"

Before you initiate any hiring activity, I highly recommend that you spend some time with your human resources manager or your internal or external legal counsel to bring you up to date on all historical and current legal requirements passed by federal, state, or local lawmakers. These may seem like unnecessary nuisances, but they have been made into laws as the result of past inequalities in the workplace. You and your company are legally bound to abide by them.

As you continue your search for the perfect salesperson, you can now move into the interviewing process with a collection of prequalified applications. This stage requires you to think with your *heart* and your *head*. Don't underestimate your "gut" feelings, but try to analyze why these feelings exist.

Having received résumés and applications, you can now telephone the candidates to set up a preliminary telephone interview. Don't interview them on the first telephone call. Just set a next call date and time to give them a chance to collect their thoughts and necessary documentation. On the next telephone call, you can begin to eliminate those who obviously can't meet the requirements. *Don't go into great details about the company or the job.* Just have a friendly chat to determine the candidates' perception of which of their professional skills they might apply to the sales position. This will help you measure their understanding of, and familiarity with, the role. When, and if, they pass this telephone interview, you move on to the next step—preferably a face-to-face interview.

In preparation for any and every interview, you must collect and review three important documents. They are:

   1. *The Résumé.* The résumé is the candidate's view of his accomplishments with a subjective twist; it is a reflection of the writer in more ways than one. Pay attention to this document; it has great value. Is it bombastic and grandiose or factual and detail oriented? Is it congruent with the speech patterns of the applicant or does it appear to have been written by someone else? Is it clean and professional in appearance or dog-eared and worn? Most important, is the information complete or are there missing dates and details? Regard the résumé as something from which to develop interview questions.

Do not disregard personal and professional references listed on the résumé. Of course they are stacked in the candidate's favor, but call them anyway. Ask questions and listen for pauses and hesitations. These can give you something to focus on during the interview process.

2. *Your Job Description.* The job description document should state very clearly, and in detail, the requirements for the job. This helps avoid the halo or horns effect where you like or dislike someone regardless of the requirements of the job. Items that should be included are:

- Territory size and unique characteristics

- Quota (soft and hard)

- Daily activities

- Reporting responsibility

- Expense management responsibility

3. *Profile of Successful Applicant.* Your profile of the successful salesperson is an objective matrix that matches your own personal objective criteria. By grading the matrix on a 1 to 5 scale, you will be able to map objectively what you are looking for and avoid measuring one candidate against another. Measuring one candidate against another could lead you to select one that is the better of two less than ideal choices.

Now you are ready to begin the actual interview process. You should interview as early in the morning as possible and during the early part of the week. This will allow you and the candidate to concentrate on the interview before the stress of business begins to build. Interview in a comfortable location that has a minimum of distractions. *Never, under any circumstances, interview in a hotel room, even if it is a suite.* You can't tell how this location may be viewed by participants in a possible future legal action.

First Interview

A big-picture view is the concept behind the first interview. This is an interview that typically lasts around thirty minutes and is intended to allow you to narrow down the field of candidates. *Do not* waste the time talking about your company or the actual job. Spend the thirty minutes finding out about the candidate's world, self-presentation, and any missing or confusing details on the résumé. Listen with your eyes as well as your ears. Watch the candidate's body language to identify areas of stress and try to determine the cause. Also watch for body language that doesn't match what the person is saying. In addition, focus on areas where the candidate has generalized or uses undefined slang (such as "and so on" or "you know how it is"). Ask yourself, is this the type of person I would like to have selling to me? What would the sales team think of her? What would the customers think about her? How would she be received by company leadership and the departmental personnel she will be required to interact with?

Second Interview

Here you begin to discuss the generalities of the sales job with the person to determine his feelings on specific required activities. Do not go into detail about the job or your company yet. If you do, you are giving proprietary information to someone who may not really be that interested in changing jobs or, worse yet, someone who will become disgruntled later when you do not select him for the position. One of the best steps to take at this stage is to have a peer interview the candidate. Some organizations like to have other sales team members interview the candidate. This method certainly emphasizes the importance of the evaluation process to those who are actually doing the job, but it is sometimes hard to identify hidden agendas and limited perspective. Whichever person you select to do this stage of the interviewing process, make sure that he or she has an understanding of the three documents we talked about earlier—the résumé, job description, and profile. Ask for constructive feedback.

Third Interview

This round is the final interview. Discuss the details of the job with the candidate and educate her about the organization as a whole. Share with her your vision for the future. *One very important note.* Show the potential new hire the documents that will be used to evaluate her during the probationary and annual appraisal periods. Make sure that she has a clear understanding of what will be expected of her if she is hired. This is critical for success and could have some legal ramifications later if the person does not work out.

You might consider taking the candidate offsite with other sales personnel for a very subjective interview. Check first with your HR department to see if this is acceptable from an insurance risk perspective. If it is, this will be the time to evaluate how well the candidate will fit into your sales organization and the culture of the company. See if she can "close" you and the team on her being the best choice.

Final Details

You are almost home. Now is the time to demonstrate your professionalism to all those around you. Make sure there are no false or unclear expectations about the job or the candidate. Make the offer as soon as possible. Present it in person or overnight it to demonstrate how important this is to you and your company. Send it early in the week and set an expected time for a written acceptance (twenty-four to forty-eight hours). Never let a candidate have the weekend to think about it, since one's current job never looks as bleak when one is at home sitting in the back yard with a glass of iced tea.

You and the candidate should be prepared for a counteroffer from the candidate's present employer. Take it seriously and have your own plan to counter it.

Close the Deal

You've done your job well. The offer has been made and accepted in writing. Now confirm the start date and be there to receive the new hire on his first day on the job. Don't lose him now. Have all the computers and telephones ready, and walk the candidate around to introduce him to his new team-mates. **Celebrate everyone's success!**

Understanding the Legal and Ethical Ramifications of Recruiting and Hiring

This chapter started off with a warning. Now we close with the same warning. This is very important! Make sure you have a clear understanding of the latest legal requirements regarding hiring practices. The rules seem to change constantly and are not always easy to interpret.

As the sales manager, and as a representative of your organization, you must actively support the adherence to all legal guidelines regarding employment practices. These laws and regulations were put in place to prevent some past questionable practices, and they have long-term positive outcomes for all parties involved. It is, however, impossible for you to keep current on all regulatory changes. Before you begin any hiring activity, please contact one or more of the following:

- Your own human resources department

- Internal legal services

- Outside contracted legal or employment support

- Local governmental agencies

- State governmental agencies

- Federal governmental agencies

If you are planning to hire sales professionals internationally, make an extra effort to understand the legal hiring practices of the local country. The U.S. government, International

Chamber of Commerce (ICC), local country embassies, consulate offices, and specialized consultants can help with these issues.

One final note: hiring sales professionals for your team has an impact far beyond the limits of your department. Successful sales personnel can enhance your department's image, and unsuccessful ones can hurt you with other departments, suppliers, management, and, of course, your customers. But the way you handle the hiring practice goes far beyond these areas.

You are changing people's lives. They have dreams and desires just like you do. As such, the hiring process becomes very emotional and sometimes turns out to be very difficult. Protect your company and yourself. Below are a few steps to take to make it a safer exercise:

- First and foremost, be fair to all candidates.

- Evaluate them against the job requirements only.

- Eliminate prejudices and stereotyping from your thinking.

- Make sure candidates have a clear understanding of your hiring process.

- Educate them on how they will be evaluated on the job if hired.

- Document the interview questions, answers, and facts.

- Do not document gut feelings!

- Watch out for halo and horn effects that may sway your opinion.

- When candidates are not selected for advancement in the hiring process, be honest with them so they can improve their efforts on their next job search.

- Treat every candidate as you would like to be treated.

- Be realistically open and honest about the financial compensation and benefits the person will receive immediately and what the future possibilities for compensation might be.

- Continually check with your HR or legal advisor to make sure your guidelines are current.

Chapter Summary

In this chapter, we talked about the search and hiring practices that are most effective for sales managers. We discussed the importance of establishing a list of competencies and attributes required for job success, and how to prioritize them.

Next, we examined recruiting and hiring practices, including the step-by-step interview process. Finally, the legal issues were brought to the forefront to help keep you and your company safe for the future.

CHAPTER 5

Strengthening the Sales Team

There are two ways of spreading light: to be
the candle or the mirror that reflects it.

—EDITH WHARTON
Vesalius in Zante

WITH THE PACE OF BUSINESS TODAY, THERE IS NO time to rest on your laurels or to sit back and enjoy the fruits of your labors. Save that for your retirement. As a sales manager in the current business environment, you must always strive to improve performance through well-defined initiatives to strengthen the sales team. The competition is either becoming different or getting better, customers are changing their wants and needs (even if they are not aware of it), your own company is changing its focus and directions regularly, and the general business context is shifting.

The Strong Grow Stronger

There are two ways you can approach this need for continuous improvement. First, you can look at the process needs of the sales team as it relates to the rest of the organization and to the customer base. This is usually, but not always, a matter for the technologists.

Second, you can look at ways to improve the individual skills of the sales team members. How can you help them perform at their individual maximum potential when the world seems to want to hold them at an average performance? Training is too often standardized; compensation plans allow for very little variation; and customers drive products and services to a commodity offering format to reduce risk. Let's take a look at ways to improve your teams.

Linking Organizational Processes

If you sometimes feel as if you're not a part of the whole organization, you're not alone. Some of America's best business analysts and writers have talked about the sales organization being a separate and distinct operation of the business that is poorly linked to the other departments. Whereas purchasing, receiving, warehousing, operations, shipping, research and development, and marketing all seem to share a sense of oneness, sales seems to be a different animal.

As much as you would like to put the blame on others for this behavior, the cause is usually rooted in the sales mentality. Since one of the greatest attributes of successful salespeople is creativity, they will probably describe themselves in much the same way as other creative people describe themselves. When you ask a painter how he painted a great painting, he will tell you that's just what he does—he is an artist. This response really doesn't help us understand what he did to be successful. The same goes for salespeople. When asked how they achieved a great sale, they probably say it is just what they do—they are great salespeople.

The result is an organization that has very little understanding of the sales process or of how hard a salesperson must work to reach the pinnacle of success. Sales processes are very rarely linked to the rest of the organization, nor is the rest of the organization linked to the sales process. If you are to achieve great things as a sales manager, you must integrate your sales team into the overall operations of the business, just as you have linked your sales effort into the overall operation of your customer's business. Let's explore some areas.

Selecting and Implementing Critical Technologies

Any printed discussion of technologies is skating on thin ice. At the current pace of development, by the time this book comes off the press, technologies will probably have evolved into something new. There are, though, some things to consider.

- Technology has never made a poor salesperson a better one. If a salesperson doesn't have it in him or her to sell, technology won't help.

- Next, your information technology department or IT vendor should *not* be the one to select the technology for the sales organization. That does not mean the people in IT don't know their job. They just don't know your sales job. Their world is very different from the typical sales world, and they need proactive guidance from the sales team.

- Never implement technology just to look sophisticated. Make sure it has some benefit for the sales personnel and for the targeted customer base.

- Never implement technology that will place such demands on the sales personnel that they will have less time to sell. Focus instead on technologies that will give them more time to do what they do best.

- Always stay alert to what the competition is deploying in technology. That doesn't mean you must follow it. Evaluate it carefully and determine its strengths and weaknesses.

- Always explore the technologies that your target market segment is deploying to identify opportunities for connectivity.

- Look for technologies that are evolutionary, not revolutionary.

As you look for technologies to implement, consider the personality preferences and values of your team members. They are not all at the same stage of technology acceptance. Allow for some small variations.

Understanding Evolving Technologies and Software

Technology can mean a lot of different things to a lot of different people. For the purposes of the discussion, we'll refer to two primary areas: software and hardware and transmission media.

The software/hardware configuration is becoming a less visible part of our technological world. It was around 1984 that desktop computers were first deployed across the general business environment and became a tool of sales forces everywhere, usually in the early applications of proposal writing and spreadsheet analysis. They were incredible machines for their time, but somewhat limited. Exact lines of words, special codes, and odd assortments of characters were required to direct the computer to do a specific task. Its predictability and reliability were sometimes difficult to align with human thinking.

Just a few years later, desktop computers are in their last generations and will become extinct in the next couple of years. Their offspring, the laptop or portable computer, is within a few more generations of seeing its demise. At the time of this writing, the personal digital assistant, or PDA, is taking over many of the sales support roles performed by its predecessors. But there is something coming over the horizon that will probably replace much of what you know today.

If you look at the history of analysis and communications, the primary role of computers, the major leaps were the interfaces available to the human user. Certainly when humans were first able to record their thoughts by applying charcoal or pigments to cave walls, it was a great leap forward. Data, in the form of animal drawings and handprints (probably recording group or family members), could be stored and was not so reliant on memory and word of mouth.

Even though these cave walls eventually became rock or clay tablets, their usefulness was based on their staying in one piece. If you dropped a record of the data, it might all shatter away, limiting its effectiveness. The invention of early rice papers and papyrus, along with writing devices, greatly advanced the control and flow of information. This newfound ability to store data on something that could be conveniently moved around was the next generation of mobility (sound familiar?). Data could be recorded, rolled up, and transported on the nearest caravan.

When the QWERTY keyboard, the standard keyboard we all know, was developed, humans had a consistent method for interfacing with a machine to record and communicate. As a matter of fact, it was so good that it made the transition from the mechanical world of typewriters to the electronic world of computers.

The next big leap was the graphical user interfaces and the associated mouse. No longer linked to command lines based on another's reasoning, users could begin to personalize their movements. Rather than the old DOS lines of command, all that was now required was to move a cursor across the screen and click on a cute little character icon. All the necessary commands were hidden out of sight. Computers became user friendly.

We are now at the next stage of human to machine interactions: voice recognition. Voice recognition has been limited by the size of memory chips that would store the algorithms to not only remember the meanings of words, but to make assumptions as to the intent of the meaning. For example, if someone spoke the phrase "bare facts," it could be recognized in diverse contextual formats that would have several different meanings. Until very recently, chips could store only enough variations to capture a few individual slang words and accents. This is no longer true. Voice recognition systems, along with proximity devices, are available today that will move technology in a whole new direction. Users will, for the first time, not be required to be physically connected to a "box." Once there is no longer a physical connection, why do we need a computer in our sight at all? Let's move it out of view and incorporate it into the Internet. Then, anywhere we go, an environment will recognize us and provide all the intelligence necessary for daily business and personal activities.

One interesting side effect of this new virtual computing reality is that those who hate or dread computers and technology will no longer find the need to use them. They will just speak to a familiar and user-friendly environment that has been personalized to feel more like a friend than an electronic device.

When you combine the three elements of voice recognition, the Internet, and wireless technology, you have the basis for the dream technology for sales organizations.

1. **Voice recognition = Personalization of computing**

2. **Internet = Unlimited information**

3. **Wireless technology = Mobility**

Sales professionals, within the very near future, will have personalized accessibility to all pertinent information stored across the Internet, irrespective of where they are or when they might need it. For all intents and purposes, the technology will be invisible since you will no longer require a linkage to physical hardware. Office buildings, public places, and private residences will all be connected to the Internet—*all the time.* All sales professionals will need to do is identify themselves (verbally or through a personal identifier proximity chip) and request data that they will then filter into the information required to make wise choices.

How this is organized and stored, though, will become more a matter of the software sciences. This, too, is a rapidly evolving field. Let's take a look at three variations of software that could and will impact the sales team.

1. *Contact Management Software (CMS).* This software has been around for a while and has evolved from a hardware-based program to a shared Internet-based program. The concept behind it is to capture as much information about customer interactions as possible. From very simple to very complex, these packages collect and organize information on customer profiles, previous contact data, future contact schedules and expectations, sales, pricing, and other issues.

CMS may, if sophisticated enough, help sales professionals analyze and prioritize their territory. Individual results can also be blended with the CMS results of other salespeople to help the sales manager improve performance and forecast results and to provide senior managers and executives with pertinent and timely sales information.

2. *Customer Relationship Management Software (CRM).* A more recent development in software for the sales profes-

sional has been the growth of the CRM programs. This is a major advance over contact management software because of its ability to link key customer processes across the organization to enhance the level of customer intimacy. For the first time, sales professionals have access to all interactions that have occurred between their customers and their company. For example, they can see the usual contact management information and, in addition, gather data on their customers' interactions with their service, finance, and customer care departments. Additionally, they can connect sales with marketing campaigns, advertising, etc.

This modular software allows an organization the opportunity to purchase and deploy only the pertinent modules required at the time, thereby providing a financial savings that links to usability. At a future date, additional modules may be added when deemed beneficial.

3. *Enterprise-Wide Software.* The top end of the spectrum is enterprise-wide software. This very advanced software connects all parts of the business, including sales, to measure performance and plan more effectively for resource requirements. In essence, for the first time, all departments of an organization can be linked to a common platform for analysis and exchange of key information.

Although not thought of as a sales software, most of the programs have sales modules that link exceptionally well with the rest of the organization. No longer will the sales department be considered a separate and distinct organization, but one that is now linked strategically to all components of the business.

Using Technology as a Point of Differentiation

As mentioned earlier in this chapter, there are several good reasons not to implement new technologies. The truth is, though, that there are several great reasons to do just that. Some benefits include:

- The need to cut through an overwhelming amount of information to get to the knowledge you need to be successful in sales

- The need to keep up with advancements in your products and applications that are coming faster and faster

- The increasing number of virtual or home-based offices

- National sales organizations that cross different time zones and geographies

- Global sales that involve different cultural perspectives and languages

When selecting a sales force technology, one question is crucial: Will this hardware or software help differentiate my sales team and my company in the eyes of the customer? If yes, proceed with your analysis. If no, reconsider.

When asking for help from your IT organization, have the answers to these questions ready to make more efficient use of their invested time:

- What information would help the sales personnel to be more successful?

- How would the sales personnel prefer to receive that information?

■ Are there limitations or restrictions the IT folks need to know?

Now you have some information to take to your subject matter specialists.

Effective Development and Training Initiatives

There is a significant change going on in corporate America pertaining to the development, implementation, and measurement of knowledge and skill-set improvement. No longer is training conceived with the same perspective we had in our high school or college days, when we sat in stiff chairs and had theory after theory pounded into the our heads regardless of their value to us at that moment in time. Sales professionals know that to be successful in today's world, they must learn content that matches immediate needs and that, at the same time, aligns with the overall objectives of the organization. This has presented a conundrum for the sales manager. Internal training programs are costly and sometimes lack the freshness of knowledge necessary for external success. External training organizations often lack the unique industry or customer focus necessary for the participants. What to do? That will be up to you.

You, the sales manager, are assuming a greater and greater responsibility for the developmental success of training programs. That doesn't mean you have to go it alone, but you are the one who best understands the needs of the overall organization. Where do you get this knowledge from? *Your strategy!* Think back to the earlier chapters. First, you analyzed the goals of the organization and where its priorities might be. Next, you determined what your short-term, intermediate, and long-term goals for the sales organization should be. Finally, you developed a series of competencies and attributes necessary for sales success. With these in mind, training should be deployed to meet these objectives and goals. As such, follow this thinking:

- Translate strategic priorities into competency training.

- Have a clear vision of desired outcome and success measurements.

- Identify the level of resident competency within each salesperson.

- Place the desired training within a business context of sales success.

- Link training with rewards and evaluations.

- Develop training partnerships that can support your unique requirements, and develop programs that will commit to provide current, accurate, and applicable knowledge that will improve, and be aligned with, your organization's goals and objectives.

- Consider multiple approaches to learning (audio, visual, tactile, etc.).

- Develop a post-training coaching methodology to cement the desired behavioral change within the day-to-day performance.

- Develop a measurement for training evaluation.

Determining Strengths and Weaknesses of Individual Sales Team Members

Most likely one of your key activities as a sales manager is to determine the strengths and weaknesses of each sales team member. In performing this process, you must make sure you don't just base your views on personal feelings. Be objective. Don't base your opinions on an overall positive feeling for the person or an overall negative feeling for the person. Don't base them on rumors or unconfirmed information and don't base them on comparison with others on the team. Instead, base your opinions on the needs of the business and on your strategic plan. Additionally, base them on your short-term, intermediate, and long-term goals, as well as on territory potential and the continuously changing needs of the target customers. Just as important, base your opinions on your coaching experience with the individual team members and observed behavior and on the continuing S.W.O.T. of the salesperson.

Watch the areas in the sales process that seems to present the greatest challenge to your salespeople. Through funnel management of the sales process (to be discussed in Chapter 7), you will usually find that there is one point that gives sales professionals the most problems and that is often the point where they lose the majority of their opportunities.

When reviewing the training needs of the sales personnel, analyze their strengths and weaknesses as they relate to the specific competencies required for success. Recognize that every day the salesperson is smarter than the day before, and incorporate these changes into any plan.

Creating Individualized Plans for Growth

The frustration in preparing a training plan for the individuals on the sales team is that they are very different from one another on the outside, and even more different from each other on the inside. They have different values and belief systems, different personal and professional goals, and different ways of learning. The three primary learning approaches to keep in mind are:

1. *Audio:* Those who prefer to learn by verbal instruction and listening techniques.

2. *Visual:* Those who prefer to watch others sell or watch videos on competency skills.

3. *Tactile:* Those who want to try it out for themselves to see how it "feels."

Additionally, don't attempt to move the entire organization through a training program at the same pace and from the same starting point. They are all starting from a different degree of understanding and mastery. As such, they require an individualized plan for development that will take into consideration their preferred style of learning and the stages of advancement.

The typical trap is to choose a standardized performance model and try to mold everyone into it. This is not effective and fails to bring to the table the unique individual talents of your team. Remember, a team is a collection of individuals pursuing the same goals.

One last point: Sales managers are great at coaching and counseling (to be talked about in Chapter 8). Formalized training is a specialized skill that sales managers should probably hand off to another person. It is not as easy as it looks, and sometimes the sales manager is too close to the situation to be objective. Also, salespeople will find additional stress in studying under their own sales manager. They need a risk-free environment. Save your knowledge transfer sessions for coaching.

Getting the Sales Professional's "Buy-In"

Sending salespeople off to training, in whatever form it takes, is often not successful for several reasons. Among them are:

- They may not feel they need it.

- They may not feel it is important.

- They may think they are being discriminated against.

- They may feel it conflicts with their personal life.

- They may be afraid that their ignorance of the subject will be ridiculed.

- They may feel that they are going to be hurt financially.

Work through the process with the identified salesperson. Make it a part of his or her yearly plan, in addition to quota objectives. Take the following steps:

- Review the strategic plan with each salesperson.

- Get each person's input of the competencies required to succeed.

- Ask for each person's evaluation of where he or she is in regard to each competency.

- Ask for supportive evidence (as measured by what?).

- Tie rewards to competency attainment.

- Create a risk-free training time.

- Make sure you show how the training will support each person's personal and professional goals.

- Help tend the home fires while the salespeople are away, and make sure their customers are taken care of.

Chapter Summary

In this chapter, we talked about the two primary means of strengthening the sales team.

The first is the application of technology. The effective sales manager should not throw technology at a situation without having a plan for how it will differentiate the sales organization and the company in the eyes of the customer.

Additionally, development and training programs need to be initiated to support the overall organizational goals, as well as your short-term, intermediate, and long-term goals. These must be individualized to meet the requirements of each and every salesperson.

CHAPTER 6

Compensation Programs That Drive Superior Performance

He is well paid that is well satisfied.

—WILLIAM SHAKESPEARE
The Merchant of Venice IV, 1

N ORDER TO ATTRACT, RECRUIT, RETAIN, AND develop the very best personnel for your sales team, you've got to establish a clear reward system that is logically linked to the overall objectives of the organization. You may have complete autonomy to take on this responsibility or perhaps it has traditionally been a function of your human resources department. In most cases, it is somewhere in between these two extremes and is arrived at by amicably negotiating the needs of both departments. In any case, you must contribute to the reasoning and rationale behind an intelligently defined compensation program.

Sales Force Compensation

One of the first challenges is to create a plan that supports both experienced professionals and new hires.

The experienced veterans usually feel that they contribute more to sales success than they are rewarded for and are somehow being held back or driven to a mediocrity by the compensation plans that are capped at too low a level. And you are probably going to compensate new hires at a level that is far more than they are worth in the earliest stages of their careers.

Always keep in mind that sales professionals will sell the products and/or services in the manner reinforced by your compensation plan. This is not necessarily a bad thing since it allows you to change directions quickly just by changing the compensation plan. But, please, don't change it so often that you discourage sales production. Your long-range plan should be to provide a total compensation plan that drives your sales professionals to excel beyond what you pay them.

The challenges involved in developing a successful compensation plan are many. For one thing, money is not the only form of reward desired by many individuals. Their *personal* and *professional* goals, along with the necessity of meeting or exceeding *corporate-directed* goals, must be taken into consideration. Some additional forms of compensation may include bonuses, benefits, increased authority or responsibility, increased visibility, increased autonomy and independence, reimbursed expenses, or any of a myriad of other personal wants and needs based on personality type and value system.

The easy part of planning sales force compensation involves deciding how much your salespeople should earn in total dollars; the sum needs to be attractive enough for you to recruit and retain talent. The hard part is determining what portion of that total should be fixed versus what percentage should be performance or "at-risk" pay. This balance between fixed and "at-risk" compensation depends on several factors, including:

■ *The Needs of the Company.* How much of its margin can the company afford to withhold for sales expense? How is the sales compensation plan perceived in relation to other important company functions? What is the current condition of the company, and what are its long-term prospects?

■ *The Needs of the Salesperson.* What is the cost of living a quality life in the area in which the salesperson lives? How long will it take for her to become top performers if she is a new hire? What about rising medical and dental costs? What about retirement plans?

■ *The Level of Salesperson You Want to Attract.* Are you looking for someone to step immediately into a higher-level selling situation and produce immediate results? Maybe you are looking for a new, inexperienced salesperson who will have the time to grow into the role. Are you requiring the sales professional to have any preexisting knowledge or experience, such as certain degrees or certifications?

■ *The Salesperson's Ability to Influence the Sale.* Is the sales professional going to be required to service existing and well-established customers or will he be required to have highly refined selling skills to open new customer doors and close new sales? Will the salesperson concentrate more on farming activities to grow the revenue with existing accounts or will he be more of a hunter, searching out new prospects?

■ *The Type of Product or Services Sold.* Is the product a commodity as, for example, paper towels, or is it a complete, multifaceted solution to complex customer business challenges like enterprise-wide software? What is the length of the sales cycle—two days or two years? Will the product or service require significant after-sale time commitments by the salesperson?

■ *The Specific Behaviors or Competencies Necessary for Success.* Think about the competencies required in the planning activity you did earlier. Are there any new competencies or behavioral attributes required, including technology or scientific skills, financial analysis or accounting skills, high-level presentation skills, and so forth?

The compensation plan must be clear, concise, and measurable to all involved parties right from the outset. In its most basic form, it sends a strong signal to the rest of the organization concerning the emphasis being placed on your sales team. It can define your company as having a market position oriented toward the professionalism of its customer interface team, or it can communicate an attitude of "we have to put up with salespeople, but they aren't that important around here." The company's short- and long-term focus, the value of the sales department, the value of the product or service, and the desired relationship with the customer will all come across in the compensation plan.

Making Sure Your Compensation Plan Drives the Desired Objectives

One of the most important considerations when designing and deploying compensation plans is not to get caught in a "legacy trap." More than one sales manager has found that she inherited a plan that was based on a past business environment requiring a very different set of competencies and behaviors. Don't let this happen to you. Review and ask yourself the following questions:

- *When was the current compensation plan designed?* If it is more than three years old, it's out of date with regard to industry changes.

- *What was the complexity of the products or services sold at the time the plan was designed?* Has your product become more complex with options, add-ons, or multiple applications?

- *What was the required level of customer relationships at the time the plan was designed?* Maybe in the beginning your personnel sold to buyers, but now your product must be sold to departmental managers or corporate leaders. Or, maybe it's the reverse as your product became highly substitutable from "look-alike" competitors.

- *What was the competitive environment at the time the plan was designed?* Were there many competitors the last time you changed your compensation plan? Maybe you had the marketplace to yourself at that time, but now you find more and more look-alikes that make it hard to differentiate and cannibalize your profits.

- *What was the pace of business at the time the plan was designed?* How urgent was the sales activity when the plan was developed? Had anyone ever heard of just-in-time deliveries? How many accounts were sales professionals required to service or sell to? What was the standard delivery schedule, and how has technology changed customer expectations?

How long did a new salesperson have to develop into a "producer" at that time? Has that changed?

■ *What was the utilization of technology at the time the plan was designed?* When your compensation plan was last modified, was there the overlay of technology on just about every activity the salesperson performed (pager, e-mail, voice mail, PDAs, cell phones, teleconferencing, etc.)? Remember how secretaries were made extinct by computers, voice mail, and e-mail? In the past, how much of the salesperson's time was spent selling and how much managing the flow of information?

■ *Now, what's changed?* You can bet that things have changed! Just review the business drivers we talked about in Chapter 2 and consider how much and how fast these areas have changed.

■ *Does the current compensation plan reflect these changes?* Just because "things" change, it doesn't mean your plan is wrong. Perhaps it was so well designed in the past that a natural flexibility was built into it. Maybe you need to make only minor changes. On the other hand, maybe you need to toss out the whole program and begin again from scratch!

As the link between senior management and the sales team's activities in the target market, it is your responsibility to ensure that the total compensation plan is always in line with a continuously changing business environment. There are three areas to consider. They are:

1. *Direct Compensation.* Salary or fixed pay, performance or at-risk commission, deferred bonuses.

2. *Benefits.* Social Security, health or other insurance, profit sharing, stock options, tuition reimbursement, etc.

3. *Reimbursed Expenses.* Travel expenses or car allowance, entertainment, communications, office or technology expenses, etc.

Weighing Compensation Plan Variations

When designing a new or revised compensation plan, always begin with one that is supportive of your best or most successful salesperson. After all, isn't this the way you would like all the members of your team to perform? In designing your plan, you should consider both the needs of the organization and the needs of the salespeople.

Needs of the Organization

Your plan should attract, retain, and motivate top salespeople to produce at a desired level of sales at a cost that generates profits and desired rate of return on sales expenses and invested capital.

Needs of the Salespeople

In addition to the needs of the business, your plan should supply the salespeople with a package that meets their financial obligations, gives them pride in what they do, reflects their competencies and experience, and is creatively superior to the package offered by the competition.

The total direct compensation package must reflect the complexity of the sales process. The mix between at-risk or performance pay and salary or fixed pay must reflect the general organizational objectives, the type of salesperson, the salesperson's influence on the sale, and the type of product or services sold. In addition, an effective package must reflect superior sales performance. On the basis of your strategic plan, and to meet organizational goals, look to reward those who perform at a higher level in the areas that are most important. Some methods for doing this are:

Straight Salary

■ *Advantage.* Straight salary provides the sales professional with a consistent income and alleviates the pressure to produce more and more orders. A salary plan emphasizes the importance of nonselling activities, encouraging the salesperson to concentrate on customer relationship building or servicing activities. Because payouts are the same for each period, this form of salary plan is the easiest to administer, and sales expenses are easy to forecast.

■ *Disadvantage.* This plan, by itself, does not drive sale closure behavior, shortened sales cycles, new product introductions, and market penetration or expansion.

Straight Commission

■ *Advantage.* Straight commission is a high performance measurement that brings immediate rewards to the sales professional. Increased sales means increased compensation. It encourages short sales cycles, sale closures, and prospecting to expand selling opportunities. An additional advantage is that it minimizes the fixed selling costs by linking payouts to actual sales. As sales go up, the expenditures go up. When sales go down, the expenditures go down.

■ *Disadvantage.* This approach discourages relationship building and nonselling activities. It can be a problem when there is channel conflict or required teaming. It also introduces a certain amount of insecurity for sales professionals during periods of weak sales. One result is that an organization that operates on a straight commission basis usually has a higher turnover of sales personnel.

Bonuses

■ *Advantage.* Bonuses are an excellent approach to rewarding positive actions and superior performance. If paid quarterly, rather than annually, they allow for a more concentrated focus on desired behaviors that are needed in any rapidly changing market. Some examples of a desired focus might be number of new accounts, increased product portfolio mix across customers or target markets, increased gross margins, percentage revenue growth, cross-organizational team activities, specific skills (i.e., financial, technological, or negotiation skills), call reports, etc.

■ *Disadvantage.* Many sales people feel that a bonus program does not accurately reflect the realities of their territory or accountability. This is based on a belief that the data to which the bonuses are tied are unreliable, distorted, uncontrollable, or delayed or old. Unfortunately, this is often the case.

Combination Plans (Usually Around 50 Percent of Total Compensation)

■ *Advantage.* Combination plans, which integrate fixed and performance pay with a bonus incentive, allow an organization to focus on a *group* of behaviors that will best meet whatever the organizational objectives are. The salesperson can be quickly rewarded for specific short- and long-term supporting behaviors, while feeling a sense of stability and security.

■ *Disadvantage.* This approach eliminates the simplicity of the other plans and, as a result, can be difficult to administer, understand, and forecast. One trap is that many companies spread the compensation package over too many different behaviors rather than emphasizing the most desired one(s).

Benefit Plans (Usually Around 25 Percent of Total Compensation)

■ *Advantage.* Benefit plans are not only a valuable compensation-added incentive for attracting and retaining talent, they have become a necessity for the average employee. By providing a menu of benefits, such as insurance and education packages, the organization is providing the salesperson with a highly flexible, and personally adaptable, compensation program that will meet their individual needs and wants. This program often reduces the turnover rate when it is tied to increases in years of service.

■ *Disadvantage.* The primary disadvantage to this is the cost of procuring and administering these benefits.

Expense Reimbursement Plans (Usually Around 25 Percent of Total Compensation)

■ *Advantage.* This package increases with the success of the salesperson and with years of tenure. Automobile, home office, entertainment, etc., are all reimbursed at some level, thereby decreasing the personal monetary expenses of the sales professional.

■ *Disadvantage.* This approach needs to be tied to an expense management system that encourages control of expenditures. It also must have some flexibility to be adaptive to individual territory requirements. Additionally, this compensation program requires that the salesperson be reimbursed promptly so that it does not become an area of dissatisfaction.

One other point on this form of compensation: Check with your HR and accounting departments to determine the tax ramifications of both the benefit plan and the expense reimbursement plan. In some instances, the packages can result in additional tax burdens on the sales professional.

Watching for Negative Results

Always be aware of the actual behaviors resulting from a sales compensation package. Negative results might take the form of poor sales figures, declining customer satisfaction, gains by your competitors, or other areas of concern for the business. Additionally, though, you might find some negative results within your team itself. Let's look at a few of the results of poorly designed or administered sales compensation packages:

■ *Declining Sales Revenue.* Maybe it's really a decline in their enthusiasm to sell your products or services.

■ *Decreasing Gross Margins.* Perhaps there is a lack of attention to negotiations because of pressure to move on.

■ *Lack of Broad Product Portfolio Sales.* The compensation plan might be driving single product sales.

■ *New Product Failure Rate.* Maybe the quality of order entry is poor because of overloaded schedules.

■ *Concentration on Limited Number of Customers.* There might be a limited reinforcement for prospecting or an overbalance on servicing existing customers.

■ *Poor Customer-Satisfaction Surveys.* Perhaps your compensation plan is causing your salespeople to ignore customer concerns, requirements, or timelines.

■ *Competitor Gains.* Some plans drive salespeople to look for "low-hanging fruit" and stay away from accounts where there is competitive activity. Unfortunately, these avoided accounts are usually the customers with the highest potential.

■ *Long Sales Cycles.* Perhaps there is too much of a comfort zone and not enough incentive to move a sale rapidly through the sales cycle.

■ *Inordinate Number of Failed Opportunities.* The compensation plan you put together may have driven the professionals to overextend themselves to the point of being able to identify new opportunities well, but not be able to move them through the sales process. Sometimes, they are *overrecognized* for new opportunity identification, but there is no negative reinforcement for failure to position the organization to win the opportunity.

■ *Negative External Perception of the Sales Professional.* In this instance, you may find negative comments being made by other departments about your sales team's "shoot-from-the-hip" approach or their tendency to be "yes men." Maybe your reward systems need to have some additive that will support a more positive attitude about the sales team by such functions as engineering, technical services, and accounting personnel.

■ *Resistance to Change.* This may be caused by salespeople's having a preconception of possible negative results. In other words, there will be no net under them if the change doesn't work. In most instances, sales professionals feel as if they have successfully mastered their world. Any change could endanger that success, which will have a negative effect on corporate, professional, and personal goals.

■ *High Turnover.* The plan may place too much at risk in a very volatile environment. In other words, salespeople's income fluctuates too much for them ever to feel a sense of partnership and security.

■ *Risk Avoidance.* In this instance, sales professionals resist taking chances with an account because they fear that there will be a negative backlash if the risk fails. Check your plan and do a little simulation. What would be the consequences to a salesperson if she spent time on developing a new market approach or a new order entry process? Your plan should support and encourage risk taking when it does not place the company at risk.

■ *Cross-Organizational Communications Breakdown.* Perhaps your sales team does not work with other departments. If team members fall 2 percent short of their sales objective but have made a major contribution to corporate quality improvement processes, are they punished?

■ *Secretiveness, Lack of Information Sharing, and No Teaming.* Perhaps your plan does not encourage partnering among, and across, the sales team. Do team members seem hesitant to even tell you what they are working on? A poorly designed compensation plan can cause overcompetitiveness and mistrust in the organizational environment.

■ *Anger, Frustration, and Conflict.* This is usually caused by sales compensation plans that are hard to understand, ever-changing, and perceived as being unfair.

Fine-Tuning the Plan

A sales compensation plan is not chiseled in stone. Your responsibility is to continuously fine-tune the drivers to adjust to changes in the business environment. Some of these changes might be:

■ Changes in organizational direction

■ Changes in organizational needs

■ Changes in leadership

■ Changes in competition

■ Changes in customer wants and needs

■ Changes in the economy (locally, regionally, nationally, or globally)

- Changes in resources

- Changes in sales personnel

- Changes in territory design

- Changes in regulatory issues

- Changes in demographics, psychographics, or lifestyles

- Changes in supply of product availability

- Changes in technology

Remember, though, that too many changes increase confusion and result in a sense of insecurity among the members of your sales team. Try to provide a sense of stability to the largest portion of the compensation package (perhaps the straight salary portion), and make adjustments annually to the smaller portion. Prepare a spreadsheet for each salesperson that compares what he or she made last year to what you project he or she will make this year using the same model. Determine who will make more, who will make less, and who will make the same. Determine the overall cost of sales for the corporation and its impact on the margin.

Next, try out other plan models and evaluate the impact on the bottom line. Which one rewards the right salespeople the best? Which plan meets the organizational objectives? Which plan meets your personal sales strategy? Which plan will attract and retain the best talent and drive the best behaviors?

Try out your thoughts with your sales team and get their input. In the end, though, you will need to make the final recommendation or decision.

Making the Plan Fair for Everyone

There are a few points to keep in mind that will make the plan more acceptable and fair to everyone. In selecting the right balance between fixed pay and performance pay, try to keep it simple and understandable. If the plan is too complex, it will become a negative point in the organization–salesperson relationship.

Don't compare apples to oranges. Make sure that the compensation plan is tied fairly to the realities and potential of the assigned territory. Make sure that the plan is based on accurate and current data.

Sales personnel should not be punished for problems created by other departments (for example, manufacturing, quality control, shipping, service, purchasing, etc.). When sales are down, it may not be the salesperson's fault. Carefully consider the impact of competition, economy, markets and customers, internal and external resources, etc., when evaluating performance.

Each salesperson should receive, discuss with the sales manager, sign, and return his or her annual compensation plan listing potential for salary, commission, bonus, expense reimbursement, and benefits. I am not talking about getting around to it in March or May. Do it before the previous year ends. This prevents misunderstandings and allows the sales manager and salesperson to discuss their total expense and how it relates to the revenue and margins brought in by the salesperson.

Chapter Summary

In this chapter, we talked about the necessity of developing a quality total compensation package. These packages must be tied to organizational objectives and supported by salary, performance incentives, bonuses, and benefits.

Even though there may be rules handed down by the human resources or legal departments, the sales manager still has the primary responsibility for designing the package and making the necessary adjustment to it on an annual basis. The adjustments should be made to reflect a continuously changing business environment.

The primary factors for success are to keep it as simple as possible, to refrain from diluting it with too many components, and to have an open discussion with the sales personnel about their packages.

PART 3

Producing

CHAPTER 7

Now Lead: Measuring and Managing Performance

If we would guide by the light of reason,
we must let our minds be bold.

—JUSTICE LOUIS D. BRANDEIS
New State Ice Co. v. Liebman (1932)

FORECASTING, AND PERFORMANCE MANAGEMENT to meet or exceed those forecasts, is at the heart of the management role for a sales professional. Your ability to accurately predict changes in revenue, margins, expenses, competitive actions and counteractions, shifting marketplace needs and wants, and the potential of your sales team members is the key to your success. This is based on the fact that no senior manager or executive likes to be surprised.

Sales Forecasting

As you discovered in the earlier chapters, basing your forecasts on current trends and projecting them into a future time slot can be more accurate than you realized. With that knowledge, you can determine the future performance of your sales team and make the necessary adjustment to attain the organizational goals.

Accurate, effective sales forecasts and plans involve an integration of subjective and objective knowledge and balanced top-down and bottom-up input and needs.

The sales team applies its specific micro view of the territory based on past and present trends. Team members also integrate their unique knowledge of changes within their primary customer operations. This knowledge is blended with the marketing department's macro view of market segments, industries, environments, regulations, demographics, psychographics, technology, economy, competitors, suppliers, and lifestyle changes.

The third ingredient in this amazing blend is the contribution made by senior management and executives, hopefully with the help of the company's financial minds. They contribute any changes in organizational directions or business focus, financial requirements (return on investment [ROI], return on investment capital [ROIC], shareholder value, return on net assets [RONA], etc.), productivity requirements, and resource availability. The combined result can be a disaster or a phenomenal contribution to your sales team's success.

Performance Evaluations

Performance evaluations are just what they say: an evaluation of how a person is doing against predetermined standards of success. They are critical measurement tools for sales managers, organizations, and the sales professional.

Rating Systems

As you begin the process of measuring and managing performance, you may find the task overwhelming. Let's face it—it is easier to complain about salespeople and their performance than to determine exactly what their performance is in relation to the realities of their assignments.

Begin this activity, which should be done every four to six months in today's business environment, by developing a list of areas to evaluate. Some areas might include:

- Sales results

- Sales quality

- Sales activities

- Administrative activities

- Customer relations

- Selling and nonselling competencies

- Training

- Job knowledge

- Organization

- Time and territory management

- Team contribution

- Expense control

- Cross-organizational relations

- Personal attributes

At this point, the last thing you want to do is to decide any of these areas are "poor" or "OK." You need a rating system to effectively determine their current state, where they have been, what progress they have made, and where you realistically want them to be at a designated time in the future. Determine appropriate metrics to use (dollars, percentages, ratios, etc.) for each category and *keep it simple*. Eliminate the average rating, and forget the overall rating.

The salesperson's evaluation will consist of quantitative and qualitative issues. When evaluating the quantitative areas, use the metrics. When looking at the qualitative areas, use terms, numbers, letters, etc. You may choose a 1–10 or A–D rating system, but you still need to designate exactly what these mean. One of the more common, and therefore the most accepted, is the six-level evaluation rating system. It looks like this:

- **Rating 1: Poor:** Performance is significantly below acceptable levels.

- **Rating 2: Below average:** Performance is close to, but not yet at, the acceptable level.

- **Rating 3: Fair:** Performance is at the acceptable level, but still needs improvement.

- **Rating 4: Good**: Performance is at the acceptable level with accomplishments satisfactory.

- **Rating 5: Very good:** Performance is above the acceptable level, and accomplishments are very satisfactory.

- **Rating 6: Excellent:** Performance and accomplishments are outstanding.

This is only one example. Select the rating system that is best for you and the realities of your business. Make sure that it will accomplish your desired results in the easiest, simplest, and fairest manner possible.

Evaluation Tools

One often overlooked tool for evaluating performance is pipeline management (sometimes referred to as funnel management). This time-tested method can be brought up to date with modern technology, such as the hardware and software mentioned previously (for example, contact management and customer relationship management software), or it can be completed on a simple piece of paper. Its real value is to provide you with three key areas of knowledge. First, where are the salesperson's strengths and weaknesses related to each specific sales competency (prospecting, presentations, proposal writing, negotiations, etc.)? Second, what will be the revenue at any particular time period in the future? Finally, what resources will be required to support sales at any future time period? It's relatively simple. Consider using it in the following steps:

Step 1: With your team involved, identify the *primary steps* necessary to successfully complete a sale. Don't become too process oriented and break the steps down into all the decision and exception points. Simply consider what it takes to drive a sale through to closure. Some steps you might consider include:

■ *Identification of an Opportunity Stage.* Make sure you all agree on what an opportunity might be. Typically, it must include a real need of a specific customer, a timeframe within which that need must be filled, and the necessary budgeted funds to acquire a solution to that need.

■ *Identification of Decision Maker(s) Stage.* Of course, you might also want to know the influencers, evaluators, approvers, and acquirers.

■ *First Meeting with Decision Makers Stage.* This is for presenting the viability of your company as a possible solutions provider.

■ *Opportunity to Gather Additional Information Stage.* This might be research, engineering specifications, historical data, price design, etc.

■ *Presentation of Solution Stage.* Here you should consider the proposal or presentation stage in whatever is typical in your industry and your customer's marketplace—anything from a written proposal to a stand-up presentation.

■ *Negotiations Stage.* This could be a formal event between your negotiations/contract/legal team and that of the customer or just the salesperson and the buyer working out the terms and conditions.

■ *Contract Stage.* Here your salesperson is required to actually get a signed contract.

■ *Project Management Stage.* Postsale event would require the salesperson to assemble, and perhaps hand the project off to, an implementation person or persons.

■ *Any Other Stage.* Consider what it takes to drive a sale in your business and industry; every business is unique. Don't forget any special requirements of your leadership or management team, as well as such possible departmental or support crossover teams like pricing and proposal teams.

You will probably have six to eight specific steps that can be listed within a pipeline chart. Again, don't get so specific and detail oriented that the sales professional must spend all his time communicating to you each small step he has taken on each sale. It could look like the chart in Figure 7-1.

Note the percentages at the bottom of the chart and the gradual reduction in list space as you move from left to right. First, the percentages are based on the concept that as you move an opportunity through the sales cycle and as each stage is completed, you increase your chance of closing a successful sale. I never show 100 percent because something can always go wrong—even after signing.

The reducing space is based on the reality that opportunities "fall out" of the list as each stage is completed. Perhaps the customer changed direction or lost funding. Maybe, after the data-gathering stage, it turned out that your product or service was not a good match. No matter how good a salesperson is, and no matter how good your products or services are, it's unlikely that you will close every opportunity.

Step 2: Now that you have an agreed upon a pipeline chart, you can begin to manage from it by asking your team members to provide a monthly list of opportunities on which they are currently working. Don't worry about every little nickel and dime sale. Just ask them to list the bigger opportunities over a particular dollar threshold. They should give you the following information:

- Name of customer

- Product, service, or application

- Anticipated dollar value of sale when closed

Figure 7-1. Pipeline with sample steps.

Stage 1: Identify Opportunity	Stage 2: Identify Decision Maker	Stage 3: Hold First Meeting	Stage 4: Gather Data	Stage 5: Make Presentation	Stage 6: Negotiate	Stage 7: Close Contract
10%	20%	30%	50%	75%	90%	99%

- Current sales stage

- Expected sales stage in next thirty days

- Any unique challenges or obstacles that could impact the successful closure of the sale

Now your chart might look like Figure 7-2.

Step 3: Take a look at your combined pipelines for all your team members. Notice anything? Perhaps you discovered that your team's total sales results for any specific month in the near future look dismal. Maybe you see a specific month coming up in which your resources that support sale closure and implementation of offering will be overburdened. For example, will you have enough proposal writers or contract negotiators? These charts, when combined, will help you plan for the future more effectively and will communicate prospects to your leadership with a greater sense of confidence.

Step 4: One of the most valuable side effects of a pipeline chart is its ability to evaluate any salesperson's weaknesses by identifying where the pipeline becomes congested and where most of the opportunities are lost. For example, if most "fall out" at the proposal stage, than this is probably a signal to review the salesperson's writing skills or financial analysis competency. Maybe a little training would improve the ability to advance more opportunities to closure. Or, the problem may be positioning with new decision makers, contract negotiations, or any of the other key steps to sale closure.

Understanding Changes in the Territories and the Marketplace That Impact Performance

One of the great challenges is to determine the proper interval between evaluations—monthly, quarterly, or annually.

Figure 7-2. Predicting opportunity progress.

	Stage 1: Identify Opportunity	Stage 2: Identify Decision Maker	Stage 3: Hold First Meeting	Stage 4: Gather Data	Stage 5: Make Presentation	Stage 6: Negotiate	Stage 7: Close Contract
	10%	20%	30%	50%	75%	90%	99%

1) ABC Corp — Fiber Optics — $125K — Concern: Our production schedule
2) LMN, Inc. — Connectors — $23K — Concern: None
3) XYZ, Ltd. — Training — $34K — Concern: Buyer's relationship with comp
4) etc.

This is of particular importance in today's business environment, where change is an ongoing event. Both the salesperson and the sales manager must have a continuous tap on the pulse of the territory to determine what impact any specific or combined change might have on performance results. Some areas of potential change might include:

- Regulatory changes for your products or services

- Regulatory changes aimed at your targeted market

- New or changed competitive thrusts into the market

- Economic conditions of the territory

- Changes in technology

- Distribution channels

If you see a drop-off in sales, don't just jump to the conclusion that the salesperson is not performing to his or her potential. The truth might be that he is required to work harder than the others just to deliver at the reduced delivery rate. Listen to him when he tells you about his challenges and try to understand the meaning behind the words, not just the words themselves. His insights are very valuable in the forecasting and planning process because he has a sense of customer intimacy that no one else in your organization has.

As you evaluate performance, be realistic. What is the potential of the territory you assigned to this particular salesperson? Can the territory really produce what you want it to? Some territories have minimal turnover of customers, steady economies, and a fortunate shortage of competitors. Other territories may have just the opposite: chaotic turnover of customers, lousy or inconsistent economies, and a wealth of true and perceived competitors.

Some territories may be like a blank piece of paper where the sales professional is looking to develop new prospects, while others have all the existing highly valued customers they can afford. How can you evaluate a salesperson's territory? Work with your team members to develop a territory configuration that is fair and defensible. One technique I particularly like uses a customer matrix based on two areas of importance— existing value and potential value. It is an expansion on one originally developed by a friend of mine, Michael Hunter, a world-class consultant out of Atlanta, Georgia. Over the years, I have made a few modifications to it, and it now looks like Figure 7-3.

Like our other charts, this valuable tool has several steps to successful completion. Let's take a look at them.

Step 1: Determine the value of all *existing* customers within a territory. This is easy. Just talk to your accounting people for last year's sales results. After you get all of the figures, segment them into four groups from smallest to largest. For example, are they in the lower twenty-fifth percentile? Or are they in the twenty-sixth to fiftieth percentiles, and so on? Place them in the grid from right to left.

Step 2: Next, let's determine the value of *potential* customers in a territory. This step is a little more challenging, but it can be done in a variety of ways. One method is to determine how much of your product or service a prospect currently buys from the competition or would buy from you if he knew he had a need for your product.

Figure 7-3. Sixteen-box grid.

	Potential Possess 76% of Top Client Characteristics or Better	Potential Possess 50–75% of Top Client Characteristics	Potential Possess 25–50% of Top Client Characteristics	Potential Possess 0–25% of Top Client Characteristics
Existing Revenue Top Quarter of All Clients				
Existing Revenue Upper Middle of All Clients				
Existing Revenue Lower Middle of All Clients				
Existing Revenue Low Quarter of All Clients				

Another method that I actually prefer because of its ability to make your salespeople much smarter about their customer base is to construct a characteristics map. In this activity, you determine the common characteristics of all your top customers in the *existing revenue* category. Perhaps it's growth rate, number of employees, technology usage, leadership style or culture, distributed or centralized purchasing model, margin or profitability attainment, globalization activities, regulatory environment, or any of a large number of other possibilities. Identify as many of these characteristics of a top customer as possible. Next, look at the prospects or potential customers in a territory and determine what percentage of these characteristics they possess. If they have 25 percent or less of the characteristics, they fall in the bottom row on the matrix. If they have 26 to 50 percent, they fall in the next row up. If they have 51 to 75 percent, they fall in the next to the top row. If they are a real winner, and have 76 percent or above, they are in our top matrix row.

What you end up with is customers (existing and potential) spread out across a territory-specific matrix. This helps you determine whom the salesperson should be calling on to achieve specific results. For example, to grow a territory you had better be investing the largest percentage of time with those customers showing in the highest potential value boxes (identified by the number 1 in Figure 7-4). If maintaining your relationship with your most valued customers is the right behavior, sales representatives must focus on the boxes with the highest existing value customers (also number 1s).

Step 3: Collaborate with your sales professionals on such a matrix. This should give a reality check on the territory, plus

Figure 7-4. Primary targets.

	Potential Possess 76% of Top Client Characteristics or Better	**Potential** Possess 50–75% of Top Client Characteristics	**Potential** Possess 25–50% of Top Client Characteristics	**Potential** Possess 0–25% of Top Client Characteristics
Existing Revenue Top Quarter of All Clients	❶	❶	❶	❶
Existing Revenue Upper Middle of All Clients	❶			
Existing Revenue Lower Middle of All Clients	❶			
Existing Revenue Low Quarter of All Clients	❶			

it can be used as an evaluation tool for call planning and for determining how the salesperson is spending his or her time. Here are some suggestions:

First, focus on call plans. Doing so will help your salespeople make their numbers needed for short-term objectives, as well as positioning with higher level prospects for the development of accounts that have future sales potential. By definition, these companies or customers are the ones that will give you the greatest return on invested time.

Next, focus the calling plans on the second tier of boxes (identified by the number 2 in Figure 7-5). These accounts should only be scheduled for contact after making sure that the previous group of customers in the top tier are all taken care of. Your salesperson's effort here should be to move them into a higher existing revenue value or a higher potential value box.

Finally, we come to the customers that show up in the lower right quadrant shown in Figure 7-6. Studies have shown that our sales personnel spend 70 to 75 percent of their time in this area. Why? Because these folks have all the problems, and salespeople love to be problem solvers. A second reason may be that our salespeople have known them the longest since, in many instances, they were given these less important accounts when they first started out. These folks might have been the only customers who would open their doors for them. But it's a trap. Remember, by definition, these are not low revenue–high potential customers and prospects. They don't have much potential at all. Even if we did make a sale, it is very unlikely that it would ever be worth as much as an upper left quadrant sale.

Figure 7-5. Secondary targets.

Figure 7-6. Time wasters.

	Potential Possess 76% of Top Client Characteristics or Better	**Potential** Possess 50–75% of Top Client Characteristics	**Potential** Possess 25–50% of Top Client Characteristics	**Potential** Possess 0–25% of Top Client Characteristics
Existing Revenue Top Quarter of All Clients				
Existing Revenue Upper Middle of All Clients				
Existing Revenue Lower Middle of All Clients			No place for a salesperson to be spending valuable time	No place for a salesperson to be spending valuable time
Existing Revenue Low Quarter of All Clients			No place for a salesperson to be spending valuable time	No place for a salesperson to be spending valuable time

Find some way of selling to this lower quadrant that does not waste the time of your highly professional salespeople. Give these customers a catalog or an inside telemarketing telephone number. Maybe they could be better serviced through an agent or distributor. Any way other than a method that eats up the valuable time of your team members.

A final note on this lowest tier: Once a year, ask your sales personnel to take another look inside and see if anything has changed. It may be that some historically lower tier accounts have been acquired by a bigger company. Maybe they developed a new technology to increase their success. Maybe the leadership has changed and the new team plans to move them up the competitive ladder quickly. If so, they deserve to be moved out of the lower tier.

Recognizing Individual Challenges

If you use your evaluation tools effectively, you can begin to determine the individual strengths and weaknesses of each and every salesperson under your command.

Make sure you understand individual challenges that a salesperson may have and make the necessary corrections to your program. Some of the challenges might be:

- Personal challenges, e.g., illness or handicaps

- Family challenges such as being a single parent

- Travel

- Physical

- Lack of experience

- Lack of knowledge

- Background

- Professionalism

- Competencies

- Attribute challenges, e.g., confidence level, speech patterns, detail orientation, etc.

Identifying All Contributors to a Forecast

One of the biggest mistakes that a sales manager can make is to believe the forecast is between the sales manager, the salesperson, and the target market. It would be far easier if this were true. The reality is that there are more contributors to a forecast than you might wish. Let's look at a few:

- *Marketing.* What are the department's plans over the coming year, to promote or to prune products?

- *Production.* What is the department's schedule for production rates, equipment upgrades, and outsourcing of key steps?

- *Purchasing.* Does the department have a sense of the suppliers' capabilities to provide inputs to your product or services? You might sell more, but can the purchasing division buy the necessary components to provide production with what it needs?

- *Distribution.* Are there any problems or possible disruptions with your distribution model?

- *Complementers and Alliance Partners.* If other alliance partners are necessary to make your finished offering, what are their plans for the coming year?

Make sure you communicate your forecasts to all these stakeholders.

Communicating the Results to Senior Management

You now have several tools to forecast the future of sales generated by your team. What should you do with these forecasts? Communicate, communicate, and communicate!

As mentioned at the beginning of this chapter, senior management and executives hate surprises. Make sure you keep them informed of your objectives and of how the team is doing toward attaining those objectives. Don't wait to be asked. Schedule specific times to meet—not a conversation in the hall—and provide them with both short- and long-term projections. Consider them inside consultants who may have once done your job and can be very helpful. And provide backup data.

Areas of Executive Concern

- Expense management

- Revenue attainment

- Margin management

- Brand equity

- Shareholder value

- ROI, ROIC, RONA, etc.

- Productivity of sales personnel

- Highly visible events or activities

- Intraorganization operational smoothness

- Projections of all of the above

Communicate with your senior management and executives in *their* language and view the results as they relate to their overall or big-picture objectives for the organization. If you have a problem, be prepared to present possible solutions and your personal solution choice. State the reasons for your selection, the risks involved with the solution, the costs, and the benefits. Consider senior management your in-house consultant.

Chapter Summary

In this chapter, we discussed a variety of evaluation tools, their use, and what you can extract from them in the way of new knowledge. We talked about how changes in the marketplace can affect results and how to deal with individual challenges.

Additionally, our discussion led us to recognize that forecasts are based on more than just sales input and that they must be integrated into a bigger picture to be realistic.

CHAPTER 8

Coaching and Counseling

No snowflake in an avalanche
ever feels responsible.

—STANISLAW JERZY LEC
More Unkempt Thoughts (1968)

THE ART OF COACHING IS A COMPETENCY THAT all sales managers must strive to perfect. You can demonstrate, you can show, and you can threaten individuals into striving for a higher performance, but unless you can coach the members of your sales team, you will be ineffective as a sales manager.

The Art of Coaching

Your responsibility is to determine what it will take to get a salesperson to be a better salesperson, as well as a contributing member of the organizational community. Next, you need to help the individual incorporate your knowledge and expertise into his or her skill sets in a complementary manner.

There are three terms that often get confused. For the purposes of this book, let's establish some definitions:

161

- *Coaching:* A series of steps or activities designed to improve the performance of a salesperson or any other employee.

- *Counseling:* A series of steps or activities designed to correct a problem affecting a salesperson or any other employee.

- *Mentoring:* A series of steps or activities designed to guide and help a person's career growth—usually not in a direct report relationship that exists between a sales manager and the sales team members.

We will not discuss the third approach. It is certainly worthy of review, but that will be reserved for another time and another book. Your interest is in coaching and counseling and in making sure that you are getting the highest performance possible out of each and every person on your sales team.

Think back on your successful career to date. Who coached you and what did you like and dislike about certain coaching activities? At the very beginning of this book, I told the story of how my father coached me on my relationship with the "wagon pullers." I'm fortunate that he didn't stop there but continued to coach me on business skills (and life) for many decades after that. I can recall times when I just wanted to walk away from a difficult customer, but he coached me to face and resolve the problems. Other times, he coached me to take the time to get to know my customers as people. What did I like about his coaching? My father's patience. My father was one of the most patient people I have ever known. He had a long-term perspective of solutions and a building block approach to getting there.

Other leaders who have coached me demonstrated such qualities as being great listeners (and adjusting their coaching to what they heard) and being open to ways of achieving results that were different from the ones they might have taken. These people also showed respect for knowledge and diverse experience, and authentic integrity.

Other leaders who I didn't find as satisfying tended to fluctuate too much, to be inconsistent, have hidden and secretive agendas, and create an air of dishonesty and deceit.

Coaching Skills to Improve Performance

Perhaps, after planning, the coaching skill is the most important competency that a sales manager can develop. In fact, planning and coaching are the "bookends" of the job. You start by planning for improvements and then you coach those any time and all the time.

Coaching, like so much of the sales manager's role, is a well-thought-out strategy for identifying the salespeople's perception of events, gaining their support in finding a solution, and developing an agreed-upon measurable plan of action to improve a behavior or competency. *Coaching is not manipulating people.*

Coaching can be a challenge for many sales managers for several reasons:

- Fear of being too intrusive into the private world of the salesperson

- Fear of not being able to manage emotions and staying cool

- Preconceived ideas, assumptions, and/or prejudices

- Fear of hearing something negative about oneself

- Poor listening skills (*What?*)

- Allowing too short a time or being too rushed

- Wanting to be too much of the solution

Coaching can unveil all of the above, but it can also be one of the most rewarding investments of time for any manager. For a sales manager, specifically, becoming skilled at coaching can positively impact sales results more quickly than any other activity. This is true in both the field ride-along and in the office environment.

There are some well-tested and proven steps to coaching success. Let's take a look at the two most common forms of coaching.

The Ride-Along or Co-Calling Coaching Session

It's a natural tendency for sales managers to enjoy, and excel, at this form of coaching more than any other. Part of the reason is that it's comfortable to step back into an environment that, most likely, has pleasant memories for them. They recall when they achieved such field success culminating in their promotion to the position of sales manager. Don't think I'm being critical of this comfort zone. As a matter of fact, any field and sales process knowledge you have should be passed on to your team members. That includes your successes *and your failures.*

There are, however, some behaviors that will increase the effectiveness of this time and also increase the performance skills of your sales personnel. Let's review them.

Do's

■ First and foremost, always make it a positive and rewarding experience for the salesperson. Let him know that you are there to help, not just criticize. Think back to the mistakes you made as a new salesperson. Relax and have fun.

■ Request (actually require) that the field salesperson provide you with a call plan for the day you are to be with her. Not just who the customer is, but why the call is being made. This should be accompanied with a brief historical perspective of each of the account's activities and the relationship with your organization, including any customer personality issues you will need to be aware of. Ask the salesperson to make sure that his calls are a mixture of established customers, at various stages of the sales process, and new prospects, where the door is still to be opened fully.

■ Meet with the salesperson in a relaxed environment on the early morning of the customer call. This can easily be done at a restaurant over a cup of coffee and breakfast. Hold a discovery session with him about how he thinks the day will unfold and what challenges he sees ahead. Listen for any strong personal concerns that you will want to pay special attention to during the calls.

■ During your preliminary discussions, establish a non-disruptive communications signal that will let you know when the salesperson would like you to jump into the conversation and will let the salesperson know when you feel you have something to add. There are silent signals such as crossing of the legs or a shift of the briefcase, as well as verbal indicators such as commenting on how interesting a subject is or a straight-out request for the other's involvement. This is just to smooth the baton hand-off in the most professional way.

■ While still in the relaxed preliminary morning talks, show the salesperson the evaluation forms you'll be using during the day so he can understand your focus.

■ One final note regarding the early morning planning activity. Reach agreement on how you will be introduced when first meeting the customers, and how your role during the day will be explained. There is probably a clear understanding between you and the salesperson, but every once in a while it can create confusion or hesitation in the customer's mind. You might, for example, inform the customer that you are field riding with the salesperson to collect market intelligence about the changing use of technology.

■ Coaching during the co-calling day can be most successful if you don't overwhelm the salesperson. Start off with what he did well. Do anything you can to set him at ease. It's best if you coach on one particular skill set per call. For example, you might coach on the *discovery* phase or the *objection handling* phase. If you feel the need to coach on more than one skill, try to make them contiguous. For example, you could easily link *presentation* skills with *closing* skills. If you coach on too many skills at once, the next call will, most likely, be a challenge since he will be focusing more on what he should do next instead of on the customer. Remember, what you want to see is a steady improvement, not an instant matching of your skills.

- Coach on the particular skill set immediately after each call. Don't wait until lunch or the end of the day. Work with your personnel while the events are still fresh in his mind and when he can best prepare for changed behavior at the next call.

- At the end of the day, or days, spend a few moments providing the salesperson with your overall impressions of his skills. Remember to be positive before you criticize. Also, let him know what will follow. Let him know how you will document the day's activities and when you would like to ride along with him again.

- When you return to the office, transfer your notes onto a formal evaluation form. Put a copy in the salesperson's personnel file and send him a copy of it.

- Before you ride along with him again, always review your previous records so you have a benchmark to measure performance growth.

Don'ts

- Don't demand the personal time of the salesperson the night before your ride-along. Of course, there might be times when your salesperson wants you to join him for dinner, but make it optional. Sometimes she might have personal plans, and your intrusion could be adding to her stress about your field presence.

■ Never interrupt or correct the salesperson in front of the customer unless she has just given life-threatening information, as in the pharmaceutical and medical industries where a situation needs to be corrected immediately. I know this might be hard, but if you interrupt or correct her, her credibility is diminished and it will make it hard for her on future solo calls. Also, the customer will have a tendency to migrate to the highest expertise level they can in your selling organizations, resulting in your getting all the direct inquiry calls that should have been handled by your salespeople. If your team member makes a mistake, part of the learning process is to develop skills at correcting errors made in the field. This is a skill you can coach well on, since you probably remember when you made errors and what you had to do to fix the problem.

■ Never avoid documentation! This is an important function of your role and will have ramifications for all concerned. Take notes, transfer them to formal evaluation forms, and store the information away for future reference when you might be called upon to make another field visit or promote, counsel, or dismiss the salesperson.

The Office Coaching Session

This type of session, as mentioned earlier, is typically designed for management and administrative skills, as opposed to the field ride-along, which coaches selling skills. In an office session you have more focused time to concentrate on behaviors necessary for overall success. As with the ride-along, make sure you don't overwhelm the person by overloading activities into your session. Let's look at a best practices model that will improve the success of your session and the competencies of the sales professional or sales support team member.

■ *Developing an Agenda.* Always have a specific reason for a coaching session. Whatever that reason is, you should be able to connect it with your overall plan for the team that was designed to meet organizational goals and objectives. Focus on a specific competency or behavior, and try not to coach several areas at the same time. Know what you want to achieve from a coaching session and have a well-defined idea of what level of skills advancement you would like to see take place. Go easy though. A person doesn't change from a weak performer to a star overnight.

You will probably find that to coach the salesperson (or sales support person) on the administrative or managerial skills necessary for a well-rounded professional, a quiet spot in the office is the best location. Some competency areas that work best in this environment might include the importance of completing accurate expense reports, cross-departmental cooperation, time management, etc. Don't have a hidden agenda. It should be well thought out and well linked with the direction of the organization.

■ *Sharing the Agenda.* Keep the salesperson fully engaged by sharing the agenda with her from the beginning. Also, be honest with her and tell her why you are having this session, what you would like to focus on, and what measurements you will apply to the session to determine its success. Tell her what you will be bringing to the session and what she might need to bring, and give her enough advanced lead time so she can prepare.

■ *Finding an Ideal Location.* Pick a time and place that is nonstressful for you and the salesperson. Try to avoid holding the session at the end of the workday since the salesperson may feel pressure and fail to concentrate on the session because of personal commitments right after work. Also, eliminate distractions so you can give full attention to the individual. That means a private office or room with no telephone calls and no interruptions! Clear your mind and become an active listener.

■ *Restating the Agenda and Schedule.* Tell the salesperson once again why you are having this coaching session and how it will link to her performance and the overall goals of the organization. Make her aware of how much time you have set aside and ask whether, in her opinion, that will meet her needs.

■ *Discovery.* This critical stage is similar to a good sales discovery approach. If you start off by talking, you're learning nothing new. It's far better to begin by asking an open-ended question about the person's feelings on the subject under discussion. For example, ask her how she would describe the call from beginning to end. Make sure it is an open-ended one so she will continue answering for a period of time. If you listen well, that answer will be where you will find out the most about your salesperson.

Listen for areas of emotion, called "needs statements," to focus in on, since these will be the statements that express some personal value feeling toward the subject being discussed. For example, "I love our products," "the customers are a pain," or "this rollercoaster ride" are all personal value statements that deserve greater attention. Use all your active listening skills to keep the dialogue going on these expressions.

Next ask about some of the specific things the salesperson has said by asking closed-ended questions. Here you should concentrate on the needs statements in areas related to the subject you wish to coach on. Closed-ended questions allow you to narrow down the scope of the discussion to something that is manageable. An example here might be "You said your customers were a pain. Specifically, in what way are they a pain?"

Finally, confirm the questions and answers so far by restating what the discussion has been up to now—from beginning to end and without judgment. This will often get the person to prioritize or add additional information.

If the discovery session is handled correctly, a sales manager can direct the questions and answers to a point where it segues into the balance of the coaching session quite nicely.

One thing to keep in mind is your design of the questioning process. Too many open-ended questions in a row make the person feel that he is wasting his time because you aren't doing anything with the answers. On the other end, too many closed-ended questions make a person feel as if he is being interrogated by the authorities! For best results, use a 1:3 ratio. For every open-ended question, you can comfortably follow with three (maybe four) closed-ended questions in a row. When the cycle is completed, you can then ask another open-ended question and three or four more closed-ended questions. This cycle can be repeated three or four times.

■ *Action Plan.* After you and the salesperson have determined the concerns about the competency or activity, ask him what he would like to do about it. In other words, have him develop an action plan to improve the situation. He usually knows the areas that need improvement and has given prior thought to ways to enhance his skills. This may or may not include you. You can't force your way into a solution if the salesperson is not ready to accept you. He may want training or guidebooks or he may want to partner with another successful salesperson. That's fine. Just make sure the details of the plan are specific. By the way, if the salesperson previously chose not to include you and if the turnaround didn't happen, the next time you can insist on being involved.

■ *Resources Required.* As the salesperson sets out his plan of action, help him determine all the resources he will need to succeed. People, time, tools, and money are often the generic resource categories.

■ *Timelines.* This all-important step will separate success from failure. Make sure the salesperson sets a timeline to measure progress that is visible to both her and you. This needs to be done with surgical precision. Get her to "front load" the timeline and set up milestones at intelligent intervals. Front load means setting the majority of necessary activities early on in the timeline so that recovery time is built in if something goes awry (and boy, will something go awry!).

■ *Feedback Schedule.* Although the salesperson created the action plan, you will need to know what is going on. Have her create a feedback model that will keep you informed of progress against milestones and an overall timeline. The milestones are of particular interest if you want to identify progress. Also, give her a schedule of when you want to give them feedback on their progress.

Sometimes the coaching session will not be as effective as you had hoped, but most of the time it will meet and exceed your expectations. If there is a problem or if you see no improvement, you will need to go through the coaching process again. But this time, you will probably need to insert yourself into the solution and become more actively involved with the milestones. Remember, the goal is to improve performance.

Moving from Direct Command to Empowerment

I have had the privilege of working with the U.S. Army Special Forces Command. One question that consistently comes up is how to move the traditional direct command model into a more adaptive model for today's military actions. When two or three Special Forces are dropped into a hostile territory, they can't wait to be told what to do. They've got to feel empowered to make their own decisions. I believe that, at the increasingly hectic pace of modern business, the same question needs to be asked.

As a sales manager, your time is valuable. So the question becomes, when do you coach between direct commands and total empowerment? Let's take a look at a simple process flow model I created (see Figure 8-1).

Your job is to move away from direct command as quickly as possible and learn to delegate opportunities that will lead to true empowerment of a clear thinking sales team. To keep the individuals moving in the right direction, you will need to coach often and well.

Creating a Motivational Environment

One of the great misconceptions is that you can motivate people. You cannot. Think about motivational speakers. Is the company really any different after they speak than it was

Figure 8-1. Process flow for coaching.

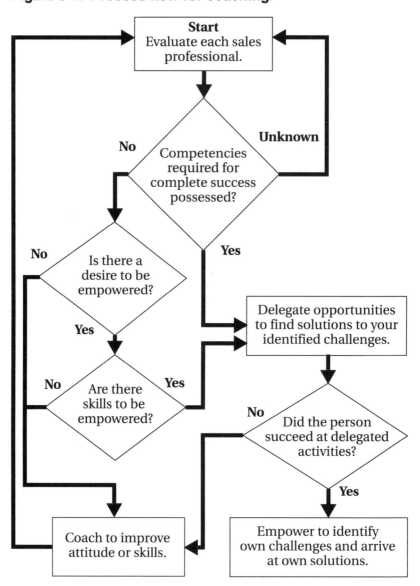

before? Probably not. The enthusiasm was based on pure emotional energy, not on a change of mindset.

It is not playing with words, though, when you say you can create a *motivational environment.* To do this, you will need to understand the members of your sales team as individuals. Find out what their values and belief systems are, what their personal and professional goals are in life. Get to know them as people.

When you do, you will find out how rich and interesting they are. They each have uniquely different experiences, different perceptions, and different objectives about what they want out of life.

Once you do this, you will have tools that will help you accelerate the advancement of individuals to higher performance. Develop a reward system that ties directly into their value system and show them how a particular behavior will allow them to achieve the things in life that they feel are of greatest value. Some examples might include:

- Greater recognition (individual or team)
- Increased power or exposure
- Spiritual or religious growth
- Additional money to purchase what they value (real estate, boats, etc.)
- Increased challenges
- Access to additional knowledge
- Travel

What do you want out of life? What excites you? Well, it is probably not the same for your team members. Take the time to find out, and document, their values and belief systems.

Dealing with the Difficult Times

Unfortunately, sales managers do encounter problems in their sales teams. This is not pleasant, but it needs to be dealt with quickly and intelligently. Perhaps the most important thing to keep in mind is what you can deal with and what you cannot deal with.

It is strongly recommended by all experts that you meet with your human resources personnel or outside legal counsel before beginning a counseling session. Find out what your legal grounds are and what you can and cannot discuss. Generally, there are areas you can counsel an individual on, but there are areas you cannot and should not get into. That doesn't mean you shouldn't help another human being, but your field of expertise is sales. Let professionals in other fields apply their knowledge most effectively.

Areas to Counsel

- Tardiness
- Lying
- Absenteeism
- Failure to complete administrative requirements
- Personality clashes
- Rude behavior
- Dress code (be careful with this one)
- Informational proprietariness
- Lack of information sharing
- Refusing to team

Areas NOT to Counsel (Follow your HR's lead)

- Alcoholism

- Drug use

- Physical threats

- Abuse (emotional, psychological, or physical)

Counseling the Problem Team Member

If you consider the areas in which you can counsel, the process is very similar to the coaching model with a few exceptions.

1. Make sure you have the facts, not just rumors, or worse yet, personal opinions.

2. Let the person know that the behavior is not just below par, but is unacceptable.

3. Make sure that you are treating all individuals the same.

4. Give the person examples, times, and places of the observed problem.

5. Show the person how the observed behavior conflicts with acceptable practices or company policy.

6. Let the person know that failure to correct the behavior will result in dismissal.

7. Watch for any indication that this behavior is based on an area *you should not be counseling.*

8. Allow enough time to correct the problem. You cannot tell the person of a problem one day and dismiss him or her the next day. Given the realities of business, the law requires a reasonable time for correction.

9. Control your own emotions and language. Discuss the subject as it relates to business and job function ONLY.

10. Document and date everything and provide a copy to the employee and to your management.

Managing Dismissals Intelligently

Many corporations prefer that the human resources department handle dismissals to avoid any legal problems. You may not have this option. If you're required to let someone go, please do it *respectfully and intelligently*. They are human beings and are experiencing one of life's great unpleasantnesses.

First, no dismissal should ever come as a surprise. If you have been counseling the individual and have set very well-defined milestones and goals, he or she should clearly understand when the recovery period is over. Don't waiver or avoid the issue. It just makes it harder in the end. Here are a few tips:

- Meet with your HR personnel first to get guidance.

- Make sure, once again, that you have all your facts straight.

- Retreat to a quiet location for the dismissal, but do it on company property if possible.

- Be precise and firm. Don't drift around the subject.

- Be prepared for a defense or pleading. If you have done your homework, these will not change your decision.

- Do not blame it on others or add your regrets.

- If you believe it will be strongly emotional, have another person standing by outside the office.

- Do not tell the person he or she can keep working for a while. This won't do any good and might intentionally or unintentionally damage your operation.

- Collect all the company property immediately.

- Document everything.

- *Make sure the person can get home safely.*

Legal Considerations

The last place you want to end up, or have your company end up, is in court because of sloppy work on your part.

I am not a legal expert and neither, most likely, are you. For one thing, between the writing and the publishing of this book, laws will have changed. It is impossible for someone with only causal interest to keep up with all the legal requirements of national, state, local, or international governments. Before you counsel or dismiss anyone, even in "without cause" states, make sure you review and understand the law.

Knowing the law will protect you, your family, and your organization from unforeseen judgments.

Chapter Summary

In this chapter, we discussed the importance of coaching as it relates to your goal achievement. There are many forms of coaching, but as the New York City police officer said to the tourist who asked how to get to Carnegie Hall—*practice, practice, practice.*

Coaching is designed to improve the performance of sales team members. Counseling, on the other hand, is designed to correct a problem. They may look the same at first glance, but the guidelines are quite different.

Finally, we talked about dismissals. These are serious actions and require the combined knowledge and expertise of the sales manager, top management, human resources, and legal counsel. Protect all parties.

CHAPTER 9

Looking Toward the Future

I hold that man is in the right
who is most closely in league with the future.

—HENRIK IBSEN
Letter to George Brandes, January 3, 1882

THE FUTURE IS JUST AROUND THE CORNER. AS A matter of fact, it will be here in a second or two. Are you ready? There are so many things to get ready for, including changes in technology, changes in demographics and lifestyles, changes in the economy and regulations, changes in customers and competitors, and changes in your own company's direction and objectives. You will even see changes in your own abilities and goals.

Perhaps one of the most important changes coming for sales managers will be the changes that occur in your sales team. It's a reality, whether you like it or not. Seasoned veterans will retire, career-focused individuals will be promoted or moved to other departments or other sales management positions, some people will drift away to other careers, and new ones will continuously be added to inspire and energize your sales team. It seems that just when you get everything running smoothly, change jumps into the picture and shakes everything up.

If you are any good at your role, as you strive to be the best that you can be, you will need to plan and prepare for these changes. Ask yourself:

- What is the longevity of the average salesperson in the company?

- Where do they usually move on to?

- What knowledge are they taking with them?

- How long will it take to find and develop a replacement?

- What will I need to do to lead this team into the future?

Let's explore what it will take to address the answers to these questions.

Creating Career Development Plans for Your Sales Team Members

A primary responsibility of all sales managers is to develop a career plan for each and every salesperson and sales support person on their team or in their area of responsibility. It seems that we become so focused on today's events and immediate goal attainment that we often fall short in thinking about the goals of our individual team members.

Matching the Plan to Goals

A goal is a vision of an end result that could or would be produced by an effort. Goals give us directions and milestones throughout our lives. Let's look at three of the most important types of goals.

Organizationally Directed Goals

Of course the most obvious goals team members have, and the ones that will support the others, are the goals you and the organization have assigned to them. They can be a certain sales revenue attainment, skills development, gross margin attainments, problem resolution success, new territory expansion, product portfolio acceptance, and so forth. If sales professionals are going to be successful in their role, they must meet and exceed these goals. But another reason for achieving these organizationally directed goals is linkage to their other goals in life. What do you know about their other goals?

Personal or Life Goals

What do your team members want out of life? A personal goal could best be described as what a person would like to achieve during his or her lifetime. These goals might include financial security for their offspring, seeing the world, contributing to new knowledge, a certain level of religious attainment, etc. Even if you believe in reincarnation (my views seem to change as I get older), you only have limited chances in this life to achieve your overall personal goal.

Professional or Career Goals

What do team members want out of their careers? This may or may not be tied to the jobs they are currently doing and the company by which they are currently employed. Somewhere in their minds, maybe from a seed generated back in elementary or high school, they have a goal of what they've imagined they could be someday. It may be to write a great adventure novel or to open a charter fishing boat service in the Caribbean. Whatever it is, they will either be happy that their present activity supports growth in that direction or frustrated that it presents so many obstacles. You get only two or three chances in a lifetime to achieve professional goals.

If *personal* goals are dependent on achieving *professional* goals, we had better pay close attention to what it will take to help people in their career plans. The result, of course, is that they will justifiably feel that we are supportive of everything that's important to them in life. To help them feel successful, we need to get a few more answers to key questions so that we can develop a career plan, not just a sales plan, for each member of our team.

■ *What competencies and attributes are required for the achievement of professional goals?* What can you do to make your salespeople successful enough to advance toward their professional goal(s)? Up until now we've been concentrating on the skills necessary for them to be successful in their current role, but what about preparing them for the future? As their sales manager, you need to have a clear understanding of where they would like to go and what it will take to get them there. Visualize the future role they have in mind, hopefully in partnership with them, and identify the characteristics and competencies required for them to be successful in that future role.

For example, if they dream of becoming a sales manager, think of all the skills we've talked about in this book that are different from the sales role. Maybe they want to move into marketing or finance. What different goals are necessary to position them for an opportunity in those departments, and what will it take to succeed if they do get a chance for career advancement in that direction?

I've even worked with a few firms that knew their direction was going to change and that most of the sales team would be laid off. To their great credit, they invested a great amount of time and financial resources in preparing these individuals to be more successful as they moved on by providing training and experience based on their individual goals. A pretty humane approach, wouldn't you say?

- *Where are they in regard to the required competencies and attributes?* After you and your salesperson have identified the competencies required to position them for, and succeed in attaining, a professional goal, determine where they currently are in the particular knowledge or attribute. Do they have only basic understanding or are they well along in skill set development?

- *What experience or training will be required to gain these competencies or attributes?* Consider what training or experiential activities you might be able to provide that will help them along the path to goal attainment. Of course, this has to be done as an enrichment activity that won't impact the sales department's goals.

- *What is a reasonable timeline for achieving these competencies?* How you structure these goal attainment activities will be dependent on how fast people see themselves reaching their goals. I know of some sales managers who overloaded an individual by trying to speed up the process when the salesperson had a much slower, longer building-block approach to new competencies.

■ *What is a reasonable timeline for achieving these goals?* For both of your sakes, be sure you have a clear understanding of when your salespeople expect to have absorbed all the competencies required and would like to move on. More than one trust has been damaged by a difference of opinion as to the releaseability (the effect on the organization of the release) of a salesperson to move to another job.

■ *Are they working toward goal attainment now?* If not, get them on it at any pace acceptable. They will be happier, and you will have a greater ability to manage for change.

Single and Dual Developmental Tracking Models

One form of career development that is growing in popularity is the *dual tracking model*. This looks at two stages in a person's career: the position he or she currently holds and his or her most likely next position. Certain competency training is required for the current sales role right now. The concept states that as the person gains this expertise, say 75 to 85 percent, he or she can then begin to take training for the most likely next position. In effect, the person is improving his or her current necessary skill sets while preparing for a smooth transition into a future role.

Preparing for Turnover

Preparing for turnover will allow you to stabilize the disruption that it causes. There will always be turnover, but some elements have created an environment of necessary change that has led to higher turnover rates. The new elements include:

- The need for constant change to keep a business healthy

- Value migration of customer wants and needs

- Technology

- Pace of business functions

- Definition of competition

- A changed relationship between an organization and its employees

- Mobility

- Demographic and cultural shifts

As you look back through the department's records, try to determine what the turnover rate has been and, if the trend continues, what it might be in the future. Also try to determine the level of experience of the departing salespeople. Were they new hires, experienced, or "old pros"? Is the ratio changing? If the results are correct, you can now estimate the number of new employees you will need to fill in for the departing ones on an annual basis.

Succession and Legacy Planning

In most cases, the departing sales professional possesses certain competencies and attributes that have made them successful. Many sales mangers, when faced with the task of replacing these folks, search for someone just like them. This is a mistake.

Succession planning is the approach taken to evaluate the changing needs of the sales assignment. Review and analyze what demands the last salesperson faced and determine what has changed. Is the competition different? Is the marketplace different? Are your products and services changing? Is the required technology different? How about size and complexity of the territory and marketplace? What about global issues?

What unique new competencies and attributes will be needed by the salesperson coming into the job that the past salesperson could get by without because of his or her experience and years of service?

Legacy planning, on the other hand, is different. One of the key findings that came out of the significant downsizing of the 1980s and 1990s was the fact that the majority of knowledge on how to do the job disappeared with the individual being downsized. Perhaps some of the first to recognize this were the managers in federal agencies during President Reagan's term in office. As they reduced headcount, their effectiveness decreased.

Organizations operate on three communications levels. The first is the formal processes built into an organizational design. These are the SOPSs (Standard Operating Procedures) or M&Ps (Methods and Practices).

The second is the informal communications that bypass formal processes to get the work done more quickly. This conversation is in the hall or at the coffee machine, and it contributes a significant amount of functionality to a business. In fact, studies have shown that this is the channel by which the bulk of the work gets done.

The third is the social network or relationships that exist within a business. Friends network and help friends. Just watch who goes to lunch together or parties together outside of work. They may not realize how much communication pertaining to business functions take place in this environment, but the amount is amazing. Consider the last time you or your associates played golf. Business topics were part of the entire day's conversation, and a lot of action items came out of the eighteen holes.

To solve this problem, excellent managers track the career progress of their sales personnel and determine when they are likely to move out of the organization. In preparation for this event, a plan is put in place to capture what these people do to be successful in their territories or assigned responsibilities. Perhaps they tutor a younger person. Maybe they document historical patterns of the customers. Whatever the process, make sure you capture what they know before they leave. This is *legacy planning*.

Wearing the Mantle of Leadership

As we begin to wrap up this book on sales management, we're obligated to spend some time on you. Are you the leader you would like to be? Do you have the necessary passion and competencies to become the leader you have the potential of being?

There are probably more books written on leadership each year than any other subject. They are written from a lot of different perspectives by a lot of different people who all seem to point out, consciously or unconsciously, that there is no single model of leadership. Compare a Mahatma Gandhi with a Jack Welch. Compare a Dr. Martin Luther King, Jr. with a Sir Winston Churchill. Some of the great leaders we know by name, while others we know by results. Consider the passionate leaders of such outstanding organizations as Fannie Mae, 3M, Nokia, Gillette, and Sony.

On outward appearance, they seem to have very little in common. But, as leaders, they all demonstrate some very important characteristics. As we consider these, let's start by looking back at you.

You have been put into this management position because you used intelligent thinking when making decisions. You weighted the objective facts, added in personal subjective beliefs, and took firm action on something in which you believed strongly. You thought about the values of the whole community of organizational members and recognized that this role is not just about you. It is about helping a large number of individuals achieve the things that are of value to them. Is leadership about being liked? *No.* Is leadership about personal gain? *No.* Is leadership about fame and glory? *No.* Leadership is about:

- *A Passion for the Job and the Team.* You must be, or become, passionate about the value of your unique role and about the desire to develop your team into an outstanding sales group. This is not just a facade. You must believe it internally as well as live it externally. Wake up in the morning, look at yourself in the mirror, and consider how lucky you are to be in the position you are in and to have control over the destiny of a team of professionals that will have such a significant impact on the success of your company, association, or organization. *Get passionate!*

- *Implementing Transparent Honesty.* If you are to succeed, not just survive, as a sales manager, you must always be clear, concise, and measurable to those around you—from your salespeople to your customers to your leadership to your peers. Pursue a behavior that is open and honest and demand the same of those around you. There can be no tolerance for fence-sitters and unethical vacillators. Business cannot succeed or excel in an environment of hidden agendas and secrecy. *Open up!*

■ *Making Hard Decisions.* Many times, these are decisions that others would prefer to avoid. Leadership is about living, and demonstrating, daily your commitment to the welfare of the entire organization through the decisions you make. *Stand up and act!*

■ *Having Consistent Values.* Don't ask others to do what you would be unwilling to do. Don't require a behavior from others that you don't demand of yourself. Know your own value and belief systems and tell the world, but do not require others to have the same values. Recognize the importance of diverse values. *Be predictable!*

Leadership is about being the kind of person that others choose to follow because they feel that what the leader stands for will inspire and create a motivational environment in which they can meet their own, the team's, and the organization's wonderful goals.

If there is one thing I have learned in my career, it's this: great leaders are not the "shiniest stars in the heavens." They can be glamorous and charismatic or they can be conservative and quiet, but day in and day out, they are consistent and predictable. They have a passion for the organization, the team, and the people around them that is easily communicated to and absorbed by others. You may find this unglamourous, but it's true. All those around you, from your management to your peers, from your customers to your sales personnel, must be consistently able to predict how you might respond to any situation. Of course, your response should strive for excellence, but it should always be based on the same clear, concise, and measurable decision-making process.

Be that leader!

Chapter Summary

In this final chapter, we looked at areas of great importance to a sales manager.

First, you can plan and prepare for the future by analyzing historical turnover rates, adjusting to change, and applying solid succession planning and legacy planning to the process.

Next we looked at leadership—what is it and how can you assume the mantle of leadership. In an examination of characteristics and competencies of great leaders, you may have settled on such characteristics as energy, resourcefulness, and being friendly and caring. In addition, you might have targeted financial knowledge, presentation and speech skills, and critical thinking as desirable competencies. Whatever you selected, you were able to develop a leadership growth plan for yourself that will take you into the future.

Conclusion

I have written this book for two reasons: first, to capture what I have learned during my long and adventurous career, and second, to address the needs of those practicing the great art of sales leadership in isolated and challenging environments.

If we talk about careers, I can honestly tell you that mine has been *interesting*. Was it always great? Hardly. Like any other business professional, I have experienced ups and downs, but I have usually found that my downs were as much my fault as anyone else's. Looking back, I realize that when I was at my lowest was when I was involved with the sales of a product or service that I didn't wholeheartedly believe in or when I was reporting to a manager I perceived to be dishonest. I know that a common belief is that great salespeople can sell anything. I don't subscribe to that theory; I believe that great salespeople are usually associated with a product or service they truly believe has value for the customer. Do you believe your product or services has value?

Other times I should have reassessed a job that I found didn't suit my personality or competencies. Sometimes I found I was not compatible with my manager. There is the reality that minds do work very differently. How's your fit? You may find that you and your manager have different styles and outlooks, but this, as I have come to learn, cannot be an excuse for lack of success. It just means that one of your plans must be to determine what values your manager holds that cause him or her to act in a certain manner that you find challenging, and what values you have that cause you to be challenged by the manager's behavior or reasoning. Then, create an action plan to build on what you *do have in common* and what you must do to make the manager feel successful in any interaction with you. Don't try to change your values, since neither you nor your manager has the lengthy time it takes to do that. Find a way to satisfy your manager's values.

I have been able to write this book based on the knowledge gained from the greatest successes and failures that occurred during my career. I usually found the greatest successes came when I was surrounded with individual leaders, or a leadership team, that was supportive and enthusiastic about what I brought in the way of solutions to business challenges. They were also consistently predictable in their support of my efforts. I would like to name them all, but I have saved several of the best for the acknowledgements at the end of this book.

One leader, in particular, though, stands out in my mind and deserves to be highlighted. His name is John and he was, and still is, the finest leader I have ever encountered. He can help us determine some characteristics of great leadership. I first met John when he was president of AT&T New Business Development, when he plucked me out of an area sales management role in California to lead One AT&T Solutions from AT&T's headquarters in New Jersey.

John was unique among powerful leaders in that he consistently conveyed a sense of equality with all those around him, no matter what their professional level. Every day his behavior seemed to add to his legendary status as told and retold by those he worked with in both the domestic and international arenas. He always took the time out of his extremely busy schedule to celebrate successes, birthdays, retirements, or whatever arose on the human side of business. He was also consistently honest with, and made hard decisions about, those he was working with, as when AT&T chose to go through divestiture (the breakup of the Bell Systems) and then "trivestiture" (the spin-off of Lucent Technologies and NCR) resulting in downsizings, relocations, and altered careers. I am not sure if John has ever understood the power of his leadership skills, but on behalf of all his faithful fans, I would like to express my gratitude for both his business skills and his humanity.

Do you know a leader like that? Are you one? Think about what you value in that person's leadership and measure yourself against it as a benchmark.

The second reason for this book is to support all the sales managers out there who don't have large organizational support structures around them. We often think of large sales teams from IBM or Dell, but the overwhelming majority of new sales managers are moving up in a small or medium-size company outside of the major metropolitan areas. This middle majority can be challenging. Sometimes the role is new to the company and sometimes not, but the dynamics of learning skills in an environment that cannot support, or afford, formalized training can be challenging. *Just don't try to do it alone.* Build a support network of others like you in similar sales management situations and exchange experiences and challenges on a regular schedule. If you do, you will succeed.

As a final note, I've constructed a leadership self-evaluation form for you on the following pages. Complete and use it for your own personal growth plan. Have a great time sales managing. It's one of the greatest jobs in the world!

A Leadership Growth Plan

Please give careful consideration to each of the following questions and use it as your personal Leadership Growth Plan.

Date: **Date to Review:**

Name: _____

Current Organization and Position

_____

_____

Personal Leadership S.W.O.T.

Strengths as a Leader	Weaknesses as a Leader
•	•
•	•
•	•
•	•
•	•
Opportunities If I Succeed	**Threats If I Fail**
•	•
•	•
•	•
•	•
•	•

Specific Weaknesses I Must Improve

Weakness No. 1

- Plan of Action (What)

- Timeline (When):

- Milestone Measurement (How Far):

- Resources Required (People, Time, Tools, Money):

Weakness No. 2

- Plan of Action (What)

- Timeline (When):

- Milestone Measurement (How Far):

- Resources Required (People, Time, Tools, Money):

Weakness No. 3

- Plan of Action (What)

- Timeline (When):

- Milestone Measurement (How Far):

- Resources Required (People, Time, Tools, Money):

A Checklist for Success

☐ Do I clearly understand what the goals and objectives are for the organization as a whole?

☐ Have I talked with my leadership to understand clearly what is expected of me and of the sales organization?

☐ Have I analyzed the current state and trends in my industry, in the marketplace, among my key customers and competitors, and in the general environment?

☐ Have I identified and benchmarked our customer's most valued solutions?

☐ Have I developed the most critical objectives for my sales team?

☐ Have I, based on the critical objectives, set short-term, intermediate, and long-term goals for my sales team?

☐ Have I created mission, vision, and values statements to support those goals?

☐ Do I know what resources I'll need to reach the goals, and do I know who owns those resources?

☐ Have I set the performance standards that will be required to achieve the goals?

☐ If I need to hire new talent, have I engaged the human resource department or legal counsel so that I understand the laws clearly?

☐ Have I considered the ways that technology could help my team members meet their new performance standards (not obstruct them)?

☐ Have I set an individualized training plan in place for each of my reports (sales and sales support)?

☐ Have I reviewed the current compensation plan to determine if it is current with the new realities and supports the desired sales behaviors?

☐ Have I set in place new or improved evaluation and forecasting tools that require the active involvement of the sales team members?

☐ Have I successfully held an individualized coaching session, either in the office or while calling on customers, for each of my reports during the last ninety days?

☐ Have I, within the last six months, discussed with my human resources department or legal counsel how to handle counseling sessions or dismissals effectively?

☐ Have I created a current career development plan for each and every team member?

☐ Do I have a legacy plan?

☐ Have I reviewed my leadership skills assessment with a trusted and honest confidant who will constructively help me identify and develop the areas I need to improve?

☐ Am I constantly celebrating the progress I'm making toward my goals (organizationally directed, professional, and personal)?

☐ Do I take the time to celebrate others' successes in achieving their goals?

☐ Am I making the work environment fun for everyone, even in extremely stressful situations?

When you've checked off all of these, and have some concurrence from those around you—congratulations! You are, indeed, a

Great Sales Manager

Index

accountability for hiring, 74
action plan, 198
   in coaching session, 171–172
advertisement for job opening, 80
agenda for office coaching, 169
applicants for job, *see* job applicants
at-risk compensation, 119–120
   vs. fixed, 114–116
audio learning approach, 106

benchmarks, 19
   customer values, 20–22
benefits, 119, 122
body language of job applicants, 83
bonuses, 121
bubble economy, 36–37
bureaucratic structure, 13
business pace, 12
   and compensation plan, 117
business practices, 37–38
business sentiment, 36

call plans, 150
   for ride-along session, 165

candidates, *see* job applicants
career development plans for team members, 184
change, 11–13
   in compensation plan, 126–127
   impact on compensation plan, 118
   resistance to, 125
   in sales team, 183–184
   in territories and marketplace, 143–153
characteristics map, 148
checklist for success, 203–205
closed-ended questions in coaching session, 171
coaching, 106, 161–163
   action plan in, 171–172
   definition, 162
   feedback schedule, 172–173
   to improve performance, 163–164
   office session for, 168–173
   process flow, 174
   ride-along session, 164–168
   timelines, 172

combination compensation
plans, 121–122
commission, 120–121, *see also*
compensation
communications
cross-organizational breakdown, 125–126
of forecast to senior management, 155–156
levels for organizations, 190
by managers, 13
media, 97–98
compensation, 113–116
fixed vs. at-risk, 114–116
recognizing individual challenges, 153–154
compensation plan
fairness, 128
fine-tuning, 126–127
negative results, 124–126
plan as driver for objectives,
116–119
variations, 119–123
competencies
benchmarking, 21
for goal achievement,
186–188
competition
and compensation plan, 117
in current environment, 32
for international market, 31
computers, 97
consumers, 33, 34
sentiment, 35–36
contact management software,
100
corporate hierarchy, elimination of layers, 13
corporate organization
communication levels, 190
and compensation plan, 119

linking processes, 94–95
needs when recruiting, 76–77
counseling, 106, 162
in difficult conditions,
176–177
problem team member,
177–178
counteroffer, from present employer, 85
creativity, 4
customer relationship management software, 100–101
customers
characteristics of top, 148
comparing issues important
to, 21
in current environment,
32–34
low potential, 150, 153
needs when recruiting, 76
territory configuration for existing and potential,
146–148

decision making, 193
demographics in current environment, 34–35
desktop computers, 97
direct command model, 173
direct compensation, 118
dismissals, managing, 178–179
documentation
of co-calling counseling, 168
probationary evaluation, 84
downsizing, impact on knowledge availability, 190
dual tracking model, 188

economy in current environment, 36–37
emotion in coaching session,
170

empowerment, 173
enterprise-wide software, 101
environment
    image of current, 30–38
    motivational, 173–175
ethical issues in hiring prac-
    tices, 86–88
evaluation, *see* performance
    evaluations
existing customers, territory
    configuration, 146–148
expectations, 12, 14–15
expense reimbursement plans,
    122–123
external training programs, 103

fear of sales calls, 3
feedback schedule in coaching
    session, 172–173
firing process, managing,
    178–179
firmographics, 36
fit with manager, 198
fixed compensation, 119–120
    vs. at-risk, 114–116
Ford, Henry, 32–33
forecasting, 135–136
    communication to senior
        management, 155–156
    identifying all contributors,
        154–155
front loading, 172
funnel management, 139–143

globalization in current envi-
    ronment, 31–32
goals of team members,
    184–188
    and assessment, 105
graphical user interfaces, 98

hardware, evolving, 97
hiring, *see* recruiting and hiring
    practices
home office, and new hires, 75
honesty, 192–193
human resources department,
    dismissals by, 178
Hunter, Michael, 146

improvement, continuous,
    93–94
informal communications, 190
information technology depart-
    ment, and technology
    selection, 95
internal training programs, 103
international hiring, 86–87
international trade, 31–32
Internet, 34, 99
interviewing job applicants,
    80–86
    by telephone, 81

job applicants
    body language of, 83
    counteroffer from present
        employer, 85
    interviewing, 80–86
    needs when recruiting, 77–79
    references, 82
    résumé, 81–82
job description, in interviewing
    process, 82
job offer, 85

keyboard, 98

laptop computers, 97
layoffs, preparation for, 187
    see also dismissals

leadership, 191–194, 198–199
  growth plan, 201–202
learning approaches, 106
legacy planning, 190
legal issues
  in dismissals, 178, 179
  in hiring practices, 86–88
  when interviewing job appli-
    cants, 80–81
life goals of team members, 185
lifestyles in current environment, 35

market of one, 34
marketplace, change impact on
  performance, 143–153
mass customization, 33
mass production, 32–33
meeting, prior to ride-along
  coaching session, 165–166
mentoring, 162
Methods and Practices (M&Ps),
  190
milestones, 172–173
money, as motivator, 114
mood of consumers, 35–36
motivational environment,
  173–175
mouse, 98

needs statements, in coaching
  session, 170
new hires, compensation, 114

objectives
  compensation plan as driver,
    116–119
  critical, 22–25
office coaching session,
  168–173
  agenda, 169

discovery stage, 170–171
location, 170
open-ended questions in
  coaching session, 170, 171
opportunities
  identifying, 139
  solving, 20
  in S.W.O.T. analysis, 18
organization, see corporate organization
organizationally direct goals of
  team members, 185
overnight shipping, 34

passion for job, 192
performance
  coaching to improve,
    163–164
  impact of territory and mar-
    ket change, 143–153
  problem of standardized
    model, 106
performance evaluations,
  136–143
  documents for probationary,
    84
  forms for ride-along session,
    166
  rating systems, 136–139
personal digital assistant (PDA),
  97
personal goals, 114, 185
pipeline management, 139–143
  side effects, 143
planning, 5
  scenario, 38–40
  for succession, 189–191
  value of, 29–30
portable computers, 97
potential customers, territory
  configuration, 146–148